A YEAR TO CLEAR

A YEAR
TO CLEAR

STEPHANIE BENNETT VOGT

Hierophantpublishing

Cover design by Emma Smith
Cover art © Blinka | Shutterstock
Interior design by Jane Hagaman

Hierophant Publishing
8301 Broadway, Suite 219
San Antonio, TX 78209
888-800-4240
www.hierophantpublishing.com

If you are unable to order this book from your local bookseller, you may order directly from the publisher.

Library of Congress Cataloging-in-Publication data available upon request.
ISBN: 978-1-938289-48-4

10 9 8 7 6 5 4 3

Printed on acid-free paper in the United States of America

To our spacious selves—
lighting the way and showing us home.

Stop. Now.

Whether you know it or not, you are at the end of your search for relief, peace, and meaning in your life. No more seeking. No more wandering. No more waiting. The peace you seek is hiding in plain sight. An open secret. . . .

Everything you need is already here, unfolding in every instant. Right here, right now.

—Josh Baran, *The Tao of Now*

Contents

Preface

A Year to Clear was an audacious idea that began as a series of questions: Is a yearlong approach to clearing (our stress and our stuff) too long? Will readers be open to the concept of clearing as a journey, like a hero's journey or a pilgrimage that guides them through the peaks and valleys of their homes and hearts? Is it possible to make a difference in the interior space of a human being in just sixty seconds?

In a culture of short attention spans and quick fixes, I had no idea if a book like that would, or could, succeed. Would my slow drip method be too light to create significant and discernible traction? Would readers lose focus, peter out, and wonder, in the words of Gertrude Stein, is there a *there* there?

So I tried it online as an experiment: I created a 365-day course called "A Year to Clear What's Holding You Back!" that launched on *DailyOM* on December 31, 2013. Participants would receive an inspirational message in their inbox every day for 365 days. Now, nearly 3,000 people signed up to go on this journey with me.

As the year progressed, I was encouraged by what people were sharing in the comments section. Unsolicited postings like these made me think that my idea wasn't so crazy:

> I have stuck with this for 40 days and, for once, have not burned myself out with go-go-go. Just drip-drip-drip. Nice!

> Not a whole lot . . . YET . . . has changed in the house, but OMG!!! I so know stuff has changed INSIDE ME! I can feel it, sense it, realize all that I am doing that I've not done before . . . Not frantically, but steadily moving in a FLOW.

> Someplace along in the 80s lessons, I started to clear and things are just flying out of my house.

I am loving your daily writings; it gentles me in an enlightening way.

Am I still resisting? God, yes! But the attitude about clearing has noticeably changed from "I HAVE to clear this ALL up or I'll feel lousy" to "I DESERVE to live in a peaceful place" to "Hey, I think I'll create a delicious feeling of calm and order for myself." . . . The Joy is in the Journey!"

I have been charting my blood pressure for some time and was concerned because it was often higher than 130. The last two weeks it has been around 120. Am I clearing the Stuff? I know that I am going more slowly . . .

[This] has blown to smithereens the cliché "You can't teach an old dog new tricks!" I feel the walls of my OLD self crumbling down in a new way.

Stephanie, I have gained so much from this over the past 11 months that I am going to be lost without you in the New Year. I've loved your Slow Drip method that has actually worn its way into my consciousness day by day.

At the beginning of the experience, I didn't know how this could work. [Now,] I am about 10 lbs lighter. The lessons made it easier for me to try small changes that let me slide into new ways of being . . . [and] I'd never have remembered all those feelings and thoughts without the journal.

I am starting this over not because I didn't get it. I totally did . . . I can't imagine a life without checking in. This can't be the end!!!

Testimonials like these put to rest any question that nourishing ourselves on a daily basis is powerful stuff—and the unexpected benefits continue to reveal themselves in wondrous ways long after the changes have been made!

Many participants were thrilled to learn that I was creating this book, which, in case you were wondering, is *not* a carbon copy of the course. Thanks to that experience, and your comments and feedback, the program has morphed and expanded. What you're holding in your hands now has many more features than the daily emails, including personal stories, practical tools, and inspirational wisdom—double the content from last year's course.

While there's more content, the spirit that infuses these 365 messages remains the same, summarized by my five *S*'s: slow down, simplify, sense, surrender, and self-care.

I love this book, and I hope you'll love it too. Together, we'll learn what it means to clear at a deep level, where spacious detachment rules and awareness changes everything. Enjoy the ride!

Stephanie Bennett Vogt
July 2015

The journey is the treasure.
——Lloyd Alexander

With all our best intentions and rich resources, why is it so hard to slow down, simplify, and care for ourselves? Why do most clearing efforts fall short or peter out? Why are we so afraid to *let go*?

Our drive to attain and succeed comes at a great cost to the soul. We are malnourished, if not starved, when it comes to compassionate self-acceptance, awareness, and care. We yearn for simplicity but struggle to find it. We ache for balance but can't sustain it. There is no time to juggle it all, let alone clear the things and thoughts that have caused us to feel so overwhelmed in the first place.

Most traditional approaches do not make room for us to feel the feelings that come up when we clear, and they make us feel bad when we fall short. These linear modalities do not account for our fight-or-flight response, nor do they recognize the energetic impact that our thoughts and emotions can have on our living spaces.

When people ask me what I do exactly when I am "space clearing," they are mystified by my reply.

"Nothing" is not an answer that sits well.

The truth is that "nothing" is what people see, and *everything* is what they haven't been able to see. Yet.

The way I work to restore balance in people's homes and lives is a bit like acupuncture—the ancient Chinese practice of inserting tiny needles into the energy centers of the physical body to release stuckness and improve the flow of chi. You could say that I'm doing the same thing when I'm clearing people and their living spaces. Only in my case the needle is *me*. What I "insert" to bring about lasting change is pure compassionate awareness.

Yes, clearing is like "needling" deep into the heart of all of our human fears and attachments in order to pierce and jiggle loose every last bit of squirmy, spasmy, unspacious stuff that's in there.

It is our ability to be detached and available that invites disturbed energies in a space to magically reorganize and harmonize. Watch a mother comfort her disconsolate child without attachment and you'll know what I mean. After five minutes the child feels all better simply because his mother held a space for him.

If there is one thing that I hope will come out of your clearing journey this year, it would be an experience of baby-step, cumulative clearing, where spaciousness and awareness rule.

This book will guide the way. All you need to do is say yes, and take the first step.

What Is Clearing, Anyway?

Most people think of clearing as something you "do" to lighten your load and free up some space. Mantras like "Use it or lose it" and "When in doubt, throw it out" are the gold standard of tackling excesses in the basement, closet, and email inboxes. And built into this view is an expectation of instant gratification: As soon I get rid of this nuisance, I'll be happy again.

There is nothing wrong with traditional methods, mind you. They are perfectly adequate. The problem is that they don't work very well to address the deeper core issues that are buried under all the stress and stuff that keeps us stuck.

Lurking deep beneath our stress and stuff is unconscious **attachment** (*I might need this someday); **resistance** (*I can't face this. . . . It's too overwhelming*); **fear** *(What will happen to me if I let go?)*; and **self-blame** (*I'm not good enough).* "Getting rid of" doesn't help us to release attachments, soften resistance, move through fear, or promote self-care. Nor does it give us an opportunity to wake up to our true nature, which shines through more brightly when we release what's holding us back.

So even if the stress and stuff gets "handled," the thoughts and emotions that gave rise to it remain and become a magnet for more stress and stuff. From the soul's perspective, whose job it is to evolve, clearing the traditional way is limited, and, ultimately, not very enlightening nor sustainable.

What most clearing approaches lack is a key ingredient: **awareness**. This is the ability to tune in to and observe an experience with the five primary senses (smell, taste, touch, hearing, sight) and the sixth sense of inner knowing—*in present time.* Feeling and witnessing a task or a stressful situation in the present moment does a magical thing: It releases stuck energy, quiets the mind, helps us detach more easily, and creates openings that weren't there before.

Add awareness to weeding out the refrigerator, folding laundry, or talking to a difficult boss or family member, for example, and three significant things happen that can change your life forever: You have effectively lightened your load with less effort (even if it's not immediately apparent in the moment); you've created a powerful ripple effect that makes weeding, folding, or talking to a difficult human easier the next time; and you've helped stop the cycle of attachment, resistance, fear, and self-blame—*for good!*

At the heart of this book is a whole new—more spacious—way to embrace this thing we call "clearing." Consider these important distinctions:

- Clearing is not a finite task that you put on a to-do list and complete by a certain deadline. It is an ongoing and **revealing journey** of self-discovery that starts where you are.

- Clearing is not about freeing up some space. It's about freeing *you!* It is a **gentle process** of releasing what is holding you back and nourishing what is calling you forward.
- Clearing is not something you squeeze into your life. It is a *way of life*. It is **daily practice** that promotes mindfulness, well-being, and letting go—one baby step at a time.

Clearing, in any form, lightens. Clearing with awareness, however, *en*-lightens. You get to choose which way you want to play.

Time-Released Nourishment

This book distills two decades of teaching, writing, and personal space clearing in a format that delivers time-release nourishment for the soul.

From short contemplations, personal stories, tools, tips, new science and concepts, one-minute practices, guided meditations, and wonder questions, each lesson builds upon the others to develop your clearing muscle and grow new habits that will last a lifetime. Each message is designed to work on you all day!

Though there is no way to predict what will happen as you begin to slow drip these 365 messages into your daily life, one thing I can say is this: To the degree that you're willing to be open to the experience and stick with it, you will not be the same person you are now. As the Buddha says, "What you are is what you have been; what you will be is what you do now."

What to Expect

The 365 daily lessons in this book are organized into 52 weekly segments. Each week usually begins with a personal story to introduce the theme, and ends on the seventh day with a **Check In** to help you review and integrate the experience.

The daily messages vary in length. On some days you may receive a short quotation to contemplate during your day. On others it may be a longer message: a new concept, a tool, and/or a hands-on clearing practice. Sprinkled throughout you'll find meditations, Q&As, stories, and testimonials.

At the end of each lesson you'll have the opportunity to **Explore** a topic with two or more open-ended statements. These are your "acupuncture needle" prompts, if you will. The phrases are designed to bypass the thinking mind and open the channels to your highest wisdom. They are not meant to be answered in a classic way, but rather to be contemplated and lived. If you take the time to answer these prompts in your journal, they will help you release some buried insights (and clutter) and will deepen your clearing experience exponentially.

Guidelines

Following are a few guidelines that will help you gain the most from this journey. Come back to them anytime you get stuck along the way:

- **Be open.** As you start to peel away the layers of your former self, not everything will make sense to you. Suspend judgment and be willing to not know. If a message mystifies you, just be with *that*. Your job is to notice and allow any "emotional weather" to arise to the degree that you can handle it.

- **Receive.** Read each message at least twice; once to get the overview and general vibe, and once to deepen your experience. If you can, choose the same time of day to read the lesson and give yourself at least one minute to "receive" its wisdom. Sometimes it helps to reread the message from the previous day before working with and integrating a new one.

- **Take your time and keep it moving.** You don't want to go so fast that you miss making vital connections. Similarly, be mindful not to be so bogged down in details that you get out of step with the daily rhythm of the journey. If you do fall behind, allow your "missing out" button to get pushed, and catch up slowly as time permits. Use the experience as another lesson in letting go.

- **Don't identify.** Most of what you'll be feeling is the release of stuck energies that come from the past, from other people, and from your (and other people's) living spaces. Unpleasant sensations usually pass to the degree that you don't make them "yours."

- **Let go of attachment to the outcome.** Set your intentions and let them go. Being less attached to a particular outcome will raise your energy level, expand your perspective, and lighten your load.

- **Allow silence.** Silence creates openings and opportunities to feel. Don't be afraid of it.

- **Have fun!** This journey is not meant to be a tedious grind (even if you do find some lessons challenging from time to time). It's meant to lift, illuminate, and enlighten you. Enter each day with ease and humor and the details will take care of themselves.

Don't worry if some of these guidelines feel like too much already. You'll get ample practice in cultivating each one!

Keeping a Journal

A journal is a lifeline and clearing's best friend. For a yearlong program like this one, writing down your thoughts and experiences can be a real game changer. Here are some ways to make journaling work for you:

- **Deepen** your clearing experience when you complete the open-ended Explore phrases at the conclusion of each lesson.
- **Integrate** your progress when you Check In at the end of each week.
- **Shine light** on the journey by recording shifts, dreams, synchronicities, and aha moments.
- **Download** and off-gas any fears, apprehensions, or emotional dips you may experience to lighten your load even more.
- **Highlight** your successes and triumphs to come back to when your intentions start to flag, get derailed, or lose focus.

Remember, this year is for *you*. Give yourself this gift of reflection if you can.

Traveling Solo or Teaming Up

There are a couple ways to go on this journey with this book as your guide: You can travel solo, or you can ask a friend or two to join you.

If you elect to go solo, it will help to have a journal by your side to keep you company. There you'll have an outlet to vent, plan, and reflect, and over time you'll have a chronicle of how far you've come. You can even adopt Julia Cameron's "morning pages" approach (producing three pages of longhand, stream-of-consciousness writing first thing in the morning) to clearing.

If you could use the support and comradery of one or two others, the Check In lesson on the last day of each week is a perfect time to connect, whether it's in person or via Skype, FaceTime, or phone. Use your time to talk about what your week has been like—your successes and your challenges—as well as your intentions for the coming week. Because this work can go very deep, and safety is everything, be sure to choose partners you trust implicitly, ones who are good listeners and allow you to be completely yourself. If a year feels like too long to team up, select six to ten of the weekly segments to start with, and continue adding more weeks as time and interest allows.

For anyone who could use the extra clearing support, whether traveling alone or with others, I have created an online resource at AYearToClear.com to serve as a home base. This virtual space is designed as a central gathering space: a place to drop in, connect with fellow travelers who are in same the week as you, read what others are saying about their experiences, post questions, and give and receive nourishing support.

There is something magical that happens when we witness each other in safe and positive ways. You'll be amazed how many others feel the way you do. And the best part of sharing your stories of triumph and challenge is that you effectively lighten the load—*for everybody*!

Let's Get Started

Are you ready? You are about to uncover the divine mysteries of your most alive and spacious self!

WEEK 1
DEPARTING

The big question is whether you are going to be able to say a
hearty yes to your adventure.
—Joseph Campbell, *The Power of Myth*

DAY 1
UNWINDING

It seems we spend half our lives winding ourselves up, like mechanical toys, and the other half unwinding, or trying to unwind. If we've learned to live well, our unwinding will be even and steady. We'll have energy to spare right up to the very end.

If we've wound ourselves up too tightly or too fast over the years, however, we'll either find ourselves stuck in a logjam that keeps us spinning in circles, or we'll unwind so fast that we'll career off the table, hit the wall, and keel over.

This book will show you how to unwind the slow and steady way. But it also teaches this little mind bender: *You are not the wind-up toy.*

Curious about what this might mean? Start by closing your eyes for a few moments, taking a deep breath, and tuning in to your wound-up self. Notice what it feels like to be coiled into a tight ball. Allow whatever is stirring to arise. It could be a word, an image, an emotion, or an experience you had recently.

After a minute is up, breathe out all thought and tension and imagine yourself being infused with spacious goodness, awareness, and possibility. Take this expanded feeling with you into the rest of your day.

When you have a moment, consider this question: If I am not a wind-up toy, who am I?

Explore

Deepen your experience of this lesson by completing the phrases that follow. They are deceptively simple, designed to bypass the thinking mind and release buried insights (and unprocessed clutter). Don't think too hard or force an answer. Allow your highest wisdom to reveal itself in these responses, and all subsequent explorations from here on:

- Being coiled into a tight ball feels . . .
- It is easy for me to experience spacious goodness . . . (If it applies, notice the part of you that is unconvinced or confused by this concept, and just be with *that*.)
- Who I think I am is . . .

DAY 2
WHAT IS YOUR THING?

Behind the coiled-up mess that is our stress and our clutter there is an infinitely spacious place one might call stillness, or joy. This is our natural state of being, but we hardly notice it because most of us are caught in a tangle of worry, fear, negative beliefs, material attachments, and endless, mechanical "doing."

So what is your thing? In what ways do you resist the whole being that you are?

Spend today reflecting on these questions, without forcing an answer, and see what pops up. And if you're rolling your eyes right about now, resisting or squirming over how cliché this all sounds, simply allow and notice that impulse.

One of the key principles you'll be hearing a lot (and exploring) throughout this book is that of observing and allowing events to unfold without doing, changing, or fixing the outcome.

Explore

- My thing is . . .
- One of the ways I resist being true to myself is . . .

DAY 3
YOUR SPACIOUS SELF

Behind all the clutter and the padding is a you that is spacious and whole, grounded and present. This self can be innocent and curious like a child, deeply happy like a dog on a walk in the woods, giddy like an explorer who has found hidden treasure, or content and complete like a grandma sitting in her rocking chair recounting stories of her remarkable life. This self lives in awe and wonder. To this self, everything looks and feels new and fresh, sparkly and amazing . . . and *clear*!

Actually, this self is not really all that new—just new to you! This new, bigger self has been with you all along, waiting patiently on the sidelines to come out and play. I'm sure you've experienced her or him in flashes from time to time. This is the self that laughs a lot, doesn't take everything so seriously, and has a lot more fun.

What are some traits of your new-to-you self that you'd like to cultivate? Is it your sense of humor? Compassion? Ambition? What are some ways that you can start integrating these traits into your everyday life in small, baby-step ways?

Explore

- Some traits in my new-to-me self I'd like to cultivate are . . .
- One small way I can integrate these traits into my daily life is to . . .

DAY 4
CLUTTER AND CLEARING
IN A NUTSHELL

I wish there was a better word for it. Because of our culture's fixation on physical "stuff," clutter doesn't come close to describing the myriad ways it shows up in our lives, much less how it affects us and makes us feel.

I define clutter as *anything* that gets in the way of experiencing our true nature and best life. Visible and invisible, external and internal, clutter comes in many forms and has many faces. Here are the three most common ones:

- **Physical clutter**—possessions we don't use, love, or need; things that have no home; things that don't get put away.
- **Mental clutter**—thoughts and beliefs generated by a fearful or attached mind; noisy chatter.
- **Emotional clutter**—unprocessed emotions, negative charge, or polarizing behaviors that grow out of the belief that we are separate.

At its essence, all clutter is a form of low-vibrational energy that sticks like a magnet to things, people, and spaces. It is this invisible side of clutter that creates imbalance in our lives and makes us feel stuck. Today, consider the many ways clutter can manifest, and how it's done so in your life.

Explore
- Some ways that clutter shows up in my life include . . .
- This is how clutter stops me from accomplishing what I most desire . . .

DAY 5
MAKE IT LAST

With all our best intentions and seemingly unlimited resources at our disposal—from container stores to feng shui cures, professional coaching to TV makeovers—why does clutter of every kind continue to grow at such an epidemic rate?

This is the million-dollar question I've been studying for the better part of two decades. Years of space clearing have taught me what is necessary to create enduring change. For clearing to last, you need to

- **Put yourself first.** No amount of containers or cures is going to make a dent in reducing the stress and stuff until you've healed the patterns that created them. If you don't feel safe, you will not let go. Clearing is an inside job that begins and ends with you.

- **Change your mindset.** Clearing is not something you "do," fix, or squeeze into your life. It's a *way of life*—a journey— that doesn't always add up, make sense, or go in a straight line.

- **Slow down.** Clearing old habits and resisting behaviors is not possible until you slow . . . it . . . way . . . down. Slow-drip efforts applied consistently over time are the real game changer here.

We'll be incorporating all three of these ideas into our practice, but for now focus on one or two to start.

Explore
- Of the three things needed to make clearing last, these are speaking to me right now . . .
- I know for sure that . . .

DAY 6
SHEDDING LAYERS BY SHINING LIGHT

You know the self? That overwhelmed, sometimes grumpy, fragmented self that has lost the ability to live fully and think big? The self that is fully padded with all kinds of protections (and stuff) to ward off the calamities which "are certain to come at any moment"? The self that feels like there is a simpler way, but can't seem to figure out where it is or how to cultivate it?

Yes, these are the layers that will be melting away this year.

Take a moment today to reflect on your experience over the past few days: What is beginning to bubble up as you contemplate a yearlong journey of clearing? Have you been made aware of any revealing dreams, shifts, synchronicities, or aha moments since you began?

Tomorrow you'll have a chance to check in with yourself more deeply. If you do not yet have a notebook or journal, now would be a good time to get one as you prepare yourself for this great adventure.

Explore
- What is bubbling up for me as I contemplate a yearlong journey of clearing . . .
- These are the dreams, shifts, synchronicities, and aha moments I've had since starting this journey . . .

DAY 7
CHECK IN—DEPARTING

The focus this week was to provide an overview of clearing and to anchor some intentions for the journey. As with any adventure, it helps to gather some provisions to gain the most out of our experience.

Take a few moments today to reflect on your goals for the year using the prompts that follow. Use your time, too, to release any apprehensions or worries, and reflect on what it would mean to feel more spacious in your home and life.

Explore

- Some worries I have about taking a whole year for myself to clear what's holding me back include . . .
- After clearing what no longer serves and supports me I hope to feel . . .
- I hope to let go of . . .
- I hope to attract . . .

WEEK 2
CLEARING MADE EASY

The longest journey you will make in your life is from your head to your heart.

—an old Sioux saying

DAY 8
CONFESSIONS OF A PACK RAT

My name is Stephanie and I am a recovering (uncovering) pack rat.

Yes, squirreled away in the dark recesses of my house I still have boxes of things I haven't seen or used in over twenty years. I have food in the freezer that is over six months old. I have a cigar box full of those tiny keys you get when you buy a new suitcase—each pair neatly secured with a twist tie.

I hang on to more Bubble Wrap and cardboard boxes than I need "just in case." I have floppy disks containing God knows what dating back to the early nineties (without the computer technology to run them even if I wanted to). Stacked neatly in the corner of my desk drawer is a year's worth of price tags for clothes I've bought . . . and washed . . . and worn.

Most people who know me as the space clearing expert, a healer of homes, a teacher and devoted messenger of hope to the clutter-weary are surprised when I tell them I am not clutter-free.

Your home may be free of all excess, or be super organized and neat as a pin, but if you live in a body that thinks thousands of thoughts a day (not all of them positive), feels pain and loss and fear from time to time, gets out of balance, or loses itself in the worries of the moment, I hate to break it to you, but you're not clutter-free either.

The fact is, most humans suffer one way or another from a condition called "holding on." Me? I was born with squirrel tendencies based on a deep fear that there is not enough to go around. Softening the hard wiring of my past is my hero's journey that involves consciously clearing one suitcase key, postage stamp, and freezer-burned lump-that-passes-as-food at a time.

But this is good. Years in the trenches have taught me that we can soften our grip on attachment—slowly and gently—by first naming and feeling the object of our stress and distress. We can release the charge that these issues hold by taking them less personally. We can change our relationship with any thing by clearing it consistently—or just moving it from the floor to the drawer—with compassionate awareness.

Yes, clearing even a single paper clip or hairball has the potential to change our lives.

Explore

- One thing or thought I know I'm holding on to right now is . . .
- Naming it here makes me feel . . .

DAY 9
FOUR PATHWAYS OF CLEARING

It took me years to break the code, to identify what could make clearing not only radically simple and sustainable, but also a powerful force for change. I call it the Four Pathways of Clearing—the keys to the kingdom of living clear.

The basic idea is this: For clearing to work its magic in our homes and lives we need to integrate four key ingredients into a daily routine:

1. Intention
2. Action
3. Non-Identification
4. Compassion

Though each pathway is worthy in its own right, the four *working together* creates a synergistic effect. Neglecting one would be like taking a leg off a table. The model loses its strength and stability and diminishes the return for effort. But when the four work as a team, even our tiniest one-minute efforts are significant and lasting.

Don't worry if you don't know what any of these mean. Today's message is just the overview. Over the next five days I will explain them in the context of daily living.

For all of you who are wired for speed and outcomes, you may have noticed that action only comprises one quarter of the work. This is where you'll be going off-road into a new way of being. Hang in there!

Explore
- When I think of what my life might look and feel like without friction or resistance, I picture . . .
- The idea of going off-road into a new way of being makes me feel . . .

DAY 10
INTENTION—CLARIFY YOUR DESIRE

You've probably heard the expression, "Be careful what you ask for, because you just might get it." The mind is a powerful generator. Intention is the pathway that helps us clarify what we most desire.

In clearing it isn't enough to engage the mind purposefully, however.

There is a follow-up step that is required once we've put our intention out into the world, and that is to let go of attachment to the outcome. When we detach and allow divine intelligence to take care of the details, we create openings, and even better outcomes, we couldn't even imagine before.

What is it that you most desire for your home and life that you'd like to shine the spotlight on this year? Can you *feel into* your desire and then get out of the way? This is what it means to clear with intention.

Explore

- My intention for this journey is . . .
- What I notice when I feel into my intentions and let go of attachment to the outcome is . . .

DAY 11
ACTION—GO SLOW TO GO FAST

We definitely need action if we want to get anywhere. As Will Rogers once wrote, "Even if you are on the right track, you'll get run over if you just sit there." If intention steers the clearing vehicle, action is what gives it gas.

Action at full throttle, however, would be like living with sun twenty-four hours a day without the balance of moon and nighttime to rest and recharge. It's too yang. When we live solely to do, fix, or make things happen, we miss a huge opportunity to cultivate the balancing effects of yin energy—receptivity, presence, intuition, surrender—qualities that are only available to us when we slow down.

Have you noticed that slowing down can actually deliver the goods faster? In what ways can you adopt a "less is more" approach to clearing?

Explore

- When I slow down, it feels like . . .
- One thing I can do today to "actively not do" is . . .

DAY 12
NON-IDENTIFICATION— BE THE OBSERVER

Can you witness a disturbance without taking it personally? Can you feel discomfort without feeding the story that created it? What can you do on the spot to unplug from a drama that is pushing your buttons? This is the work of dis-identifying.

Non-identification is the pathway of becoming the silent observer of our experience: to accept things as they are, take things less personally, witness without judgment. It takes patience and practice not to get plugged in.

Try it: If something or someone challenges your equanimity today (i.e., pisses you off, pushes your buttons), give the situation a number from 1 to 10, with 10 being the red zone of activation and attachment. See if naming and feeling the problem doesn't reduce the charge and lower the number.

Explore

- Someone or something that has gotten under my skin lately is . . . (and the number I would give it is . . .)
- One thing I can do to unplug from this situation is . . . (and the number I would give it after naming and feeling my discomfort is . . .)

DAY 13
COMPASSION—CULTIVATE SELF-CARE

Compassion, as it relates to clearing in this book, is not just that altruistic, openhearted Mother Teresa quality that we all wish we had more of. The focus here is not about embodying selflessness, but rather cultivating self-*more*-ness—as in more self-kindness, self-acceptance, self-worth. It means allowing yourself to disappoint and be disappointed; having it be okay to make mistakes and fail; setting clear boundaries.

Compassion means holding a space for yourself by practicing nourishing self-care. Only when we've fed ourselves fully can more be made available for others. Compassion is the feel-good principle of clearing. When we feel safe, supported, and good we are more likely to let go. Without self-care there is no clearing.

Are you being an advocate for yourself? What is something you can do for one minute today that would feel really good?

Explore
- Some ways that I am my own best friend are . . . (Notice the part of you that struggles with this.)
- One thing I can do today that would feel really good is . . .

DAY 14
CHECK IN—CLEARING MADE EASY

The focus this week was to shift and expand the way we clear with a model that balances active doing (yang) with receptive non-doing (yin). The Four Pathways work together to soften the hardwiring of our past, create openings, and promote a way of being that is effective, nourishing, and lasting.

If you applied the Four Pathways to sorting the mail, for example, your clearing practice might look something like this:

1. **Intention**—Set aside one minute a day for a week (for starters). Breathe into the task, and invite ease.
2. **Action**—Sort the day's mail for one minute, with awareness.
3. **Non-identification**—Allow yourself to feel whatever comes up with no attachment: notice the jarring resistance when you see a utility bill, or the judgments that are triggered by junk mail.
4. **Compassion**—Be kind and gentle with yourself: give yourself props for sticking with the task, or notice how good it feels to put the mail where it belongs.

What is one thing you could do today that incorporates the Four Pathways?

Explore
- One thing I can do today to integrate the Four Pathways is . . .
- When I do, it feels like . . .

WEEK 3
GAINING AWARENESS

At the still point, there the dance is.
— T. S. Eliot, *Burnt Norton*

DAY 15
HIDING IN PLAIN SIGHT

Do you love it? Do you use it? Does it have a home?

My favorite three-part mantra for clearing works like a charm every time. Unless, of course, you don't *see* the stuff that you are trying to release.

You don't see the things you once loved, the clothes that once fit, or the files you feel obligated to save "just in case." Why? Because seeing them would also mean *feeling* them.

Feeling the overwhelm, the shoulds, the guilt, the shame, the blame, the fears, the despair—feeling all of the emotional and energetic buildup encoded in the stuff that settles in like a layer of smog over everything.

Ouch. Yes, I know. There is more going on than meets the eye.

You see, it's not about the clutter at all. At the heart of it, clearing is not about tackling the unsightly messes, the clothes that don't fit, the emails that invade your inbox, the to-do lists that get longer by the second, the neighbor who won't turn his music down, the boss who's inflexible with your hours.

Clearing is not about fixing a problem or reaching for a solution. It is about how you *relate* to the experience. The real goodies—and where the real clearing happens—are in the space between the issue and the outcome.

So how do we pry our hands off and get our eyesight back? We begin by bringing compassionate awareness to the resisting patterns, one thing or thought at a time. In present time.

What are you noticing right this second? Are you aware of your breathing? Tightness in your body? Are you distracted by your thoughts?

Explore
- At this moment I am aware of . . .
- If I were to describe what some of the emotional and energetic buildup in my life looks like, it would be . . .

DAY 16
IN THE ZONE

The best way I know to release what isn't working is to enter that sometimes-scary zone called *feeling*. Feeling the resistance and attachment without judging them as good or bad or taking them personally.

To feel fully and completely with your six senses without getting emotionally attached to any sensations may sound counterintuitive. But so is riding a bike. How do you glide on two wheels without falling?

Feeling with spacious detachment is like balancing on two wheels. As humans we are capable of feeling deeply a full spectrum of sensations *and* not get plugged in by them. To the degree that you can feel unbearable loss, pain, or despair and not get plugged in by it is called mastery.

Explore
- The feelings that most activate me are . . .
- It is possible to unplug from these feelings by . . . (Name and feel the part of you that doesn't quite believe it is possible.)

DAY 17
MIND THE GAP

"Mind the gap." All over the UK railway and subway system, you'll see this phrase that cautions you to watch your step as you board a train. I love it because it brings me back to the only space that matters: now.

Use today to mind the gap of your experience. Whenever you notice yourself getting lost in worry about the past (which is over) or the future (which is yet to be determined), bring yourself back to the present. And breathe.

How do you feel in this in-between space?

Explore
- The times I catch myself going into auto pilot are . . .
- To mind the gap of my experience feels like . . .

DAY 18
IF YOUR BODY COULD SPEAK

Most of us spend a lot of our time in our heads. Our fast-paced lifestyles don't make it easy to connect with our physical structure, our internal organs, our heart (both the literal one and the figurative one). It's like we're one big walking, talking head.

The body is infinitely more intelligent than we give it credit for. It has a way of letting us know when we're hungry, tired, stressed, afraid, out of balance, and yet we don't listen to its silent messages until we get sick. Or tired. Or both.

With this book you'll get to rewire this pattern—beginning right now: Close your eyes and notice the sounds, smells, curiosities, and nudges around you. These could be external sounds, smells, curiosities, and nudges, or they could be internal. Allow any and all sensations to arise and exist, without trying to do anything to fix, manage, or judge them.

If your body could speak, what would it say to you right now? If you ask your body what it needs, what does it tell you?

Explore

- When I close my eyes, I notice . . .
- My body says it needs . . .

DAY 19
LOOK AROUND

Have you ever considered how much time you spend looking? Really looking?

Try it: Look up from this book for a moment and scan the room you're in. What is one thing of beauty that calls your attention? It could be anything—the light coming through the window just so, the steam from your cup of coffee undulating upward, the curve in the sofa, the rhythmic motion of your ceiling fan, a bird's song.

For one minute allow your awareness to rest on the details: the shape, color, texture, sound, smell, weight. Notice if your attention changes what you see or how you feel. Has your awareness changed?

Explore

- Today I rested my awareness on . . .
- When I gave X my full attention, I noticed . . .

DAY 20
FULL-BODY FEELING CHECK

Today I invite you to slow it down even more and do a full scan of your body, mind, emotions, and spirit using the prompts that follow. You've been cultivating awareness all week, but this is a new day, feelings change, and you're not the same person you were yesterday.

Close your eyes, and take a deep breath in and a slow, emptying breath out. When you feel centered, open your eyes and scroll down the list that follows. Identify any sensations that apply to you (and/or add your own). If you can, notice what they feel like and where you feel them in the body.

Physical
- How's your breathing? Is it shallow, halting, full, relaxed?
- Are you thirsty? Hungry?
- Are your hands hot, cold, tingly, sweaty, tight, clenched?
- Are there any knots in your shoulders, neck, back, stomach?
- Are you tired, bored, attentive, excited?
- Do you feel heavy, light, constricted, expanded, congested, fluid?

Mental
- Is your mind analyzing, chattering, multitasking, problem solving, obsessing?
- Are you feeling critical, nitpicky, judgmental?
- Are you worrying about something, or someone?
- Do you feel fuzzy-headed, clear-headed, sharp, dull, rattled, peaceful?

Emotional
- Do you feel annoyed, grumpy, stressed, overwhelmed, fried?
- Do you feel a pang of something—sadness, resistance, fear, excitement, joy?
- Are you holding a grudge?
- Are you feeling relaxed, still, steady, unattached?

Spiritual
- Do you feel lonely, alone, lost, adrift, unsupported?
- Do you feel valued, acknowledged, held, supported?
- Are you feeling hopeful, purposeful, grateful, in the flow?

When you feel complete, notice if you feel differently now than when you began the exercise.

If, for the remainder of this book, you can allow yourself to make frequent feeling checks like this one: to stop, breathe, name, and feel whatever you're feeling in the moment—without personalizing any of it—you will gain the true spirit of the clearing journey, called awareness!

Explore
- After doing a one-minute feeling check I noticed . . .
- My body, mind, emotions, and spirit are teaching me . . .

DAY 21
CHECK IN—GAINING AWARENESS

The focus this week was to practice mindfulness and presence by being more aware of the messages we get from our body, mind, emotions, spirit, and surroundings.

When we slowly drip compassionate awareness into any resisting pattern we create a tiny peephole of space that wasn't there before. This peephole becomes larger over time and opens up to a universe of possibilities beyond our wildest imaginings.

What is your peephole revealing? What changes are you aware of after this third week?

Explore
- When I am more aware, I notice myself, my home, and my life are . . .
- Since starting this book, I'm aware of these changes . . .

WEEK 4
COMING OUT
OF THE CLOSET

You must go into the dark in order to bring forth your light.
—Debbie Ford, *The Dark Side of the Light Chasers*

DAY 22
CHANGE IT UP

If I could take one object with me when I die, it would be my cashmere shawl. I simply adore the feeling of being enveloped in the delicious warmth of something so supremely soft . . . *hmm,* kind of like I imagine heaven might be *all the time,* come to think of it.

What can you wear today that would feel really good? Can you wear it with gusto even if it's not stylish or color coordinated? Try it: Put something on that is pure pleasure in body and spirit. Notice and allow any pesky judgments to float above it all.

After you've donned your special something, consider this contemplation: Wearing something that feels good effectively raises my vibration and energy level.

Explore
- If I could take just a few pieces of clothing with me when I die, I'd choose . . .
- Wearing something that feels good changes my mood to . . .

DAY 23
OUT FIT

Raise your hand if you are wearing something today that you don't love, that doesn't fit, or that doesn't feel good. This includes your underwear.

Explore

- A piece of clothing I'm wearing today that I don't love, that doesn't fit, or that doesn't feel good is . . .
- Realizing this makes me feel . . . (Try to allow the squirminess of judgment, guilt, embarrassment, or shame to simply be there without doing anything to fix or manage it.)

DAY 24
THROW OFF

Napoleon Bonaparte is quoted as saying, "Throw off your worries when you throw off your clothes at night." When you undress tonight, imagine that all the stresses of your day are being released completely with your clothes. Allow this "second skin" to be your vehicle for letting go.

If you wear pajamas or a nightgown to bed, imagine that you are stepping into a new you when you put them on. If you don't wear nightclothes, use the action of climbing into bed as your anchor for climbing into your lighter self.

Explore

- Shedding my worries when I remove my clothes each night feels . . .
- Lightening my load feels . . .

DAY 25
WEARING OR WEARY-ING?

When it comes to clothes, it basically boils down to this: Clothes that don't fit, feel good, or make your heart sing are a form of stuck energy (aka clutter). When you squirrel them away for that mythical day when you'll love them again, or fit into them, or they'll come back into fashion, you perpetuate the stuck pattern.

It doesn't matter if you've paid a small fortune or made it from scratch, if a garment is not a vibrational match to *you* (i.e. it fits, it is suitable to your lifestyle, and it makes you feel good), it will not lift and lighten you. Nor make you feel attractive.

Are your clothes a vibrational match to you? Do you wear your clothes, or do they wear you?

Explore
- My clothes are/are not a vibrational match to me because . . .
- My clothes make me feel . . .

DAY 26
BEING A-WEAR

Today I invite you to take a peek inside your closet and do a quick scan of your wardrobe. Do you love most of the items in there? Do you feel oppressed by them?

Simply notice how you feel without doing anything to fix, manage, or change anything: Notice the thoughts, the judgments, the resistances. Notice the impulse to rid yourself of some things, or the sentimental tug to hold on to others. Notice your breathing. (Is it shallow? Is it relaxed?) Notice where in your body you feel some stuckness.

Nothing to do but observe.

Awareness is the first important step of clearing. Tomorrow I'll share a simple one-minute clearing process you can do in your closet to release what's holding you back.

In the meantime, if you feel moved to release (or purge), by all means, go for it. All I ask is that you bring as much awareness to the experience as you can.

Explore

- The overall feeling I get when I look inside my closet is . . .
- Scanning my wardrobe makes me want to . . .
- I am ready to let go of these items in my closet . . . (because . . .)

DAY 27
A-WEAR-NESS PROCESS

It might be helpful to remember that the focus this week is not about the clothes that don't fit or feel good. It's not about the stuff spilling out of the closet, nor having a pristine one. It is how you relate to the experience of clearing—with no attachment. Try the following exercise. It's a simple way to practice detaching and releasing stuck energy.

1. **Identify** an item of clothing in your wardrobe that isn't working for you. It could be the pants you bought because they were half price but that don't flatter you and never have. It could be the shoes that give you blisters every time you wear them. It could be the shirt that you love but won't wear because it's missing a button.

2. **Pull the item out** of your closet, drawer, or laundry basket; sit down and lay it on your lap.

3. **Close your eyes,** and notice how the item makes you feel. In the words of Marie Kondo, the famous Japanese organizer and declutterer, ask yourself if the item sparks joy. (Remember, the task is not to get rid of the item so much as to notice the thoughts and feelings that are keeping you from letting it go.)

4. When you feel complete **put it away, repair it, or release it** with love.

5. **Notice** the effect of this simple practice in other areas of your life and write it down.

Do you notice stuck energy being released by simply clearing, addressing, or tending to just one item at a time?

Explore

- One item of clothing that isn't working for me is . . . (It makes me feel . . .)
- When I clear, address, or tend to this one thing, I notice . . .
- My closet is teaching me . . .

DAY 28
CHECK IN—COMING OUT OF THE CLOSET

Closets—the real ones and the metaphoric ones—are those dark repositories for storing what we don't want to see (or others to see). This week we used our second skin (our clothing) as a tool to help us come out of our closets, as it were: to shed light on, and shed what gets in the way of revealing our true selves.

What were some of your discoveries this week? How easy or hard is it to dress in a way that matches how you feel? In what ways do you feel that you are coming out of hiding?

Explore

- Some of the discoveries I've made this week are . . .
- Giving myself permission to dress in a way that matches how I want to feel is easy because . . . (Notice the part that doesn't feel easy.)
- Some of the ways that I feel I'm coming out of hiding are . . .

WEEK 5
MOVING STUCK ENERGY

Love the moment and the energy of that moment will spread
beyond all boundaries.

—Corita Kent

DAY 29
OPEN AND SHUT

Our home, built in 1875, is cute and quirky. There may have been right
angles once upon a time, but with years of settling the seams between
the wall and the ceiling are all uneven and most of the interior doors
have stopped closing. Many of the traditional double-hung windows
don't stay up because their pulley cords are frayed or broken.

It's not just old-house issues that have never been addressed; we also
have new-house problems too, like the framed artwork that still sits on
the floor waiting for someone to take two minutes to pull out a hammer
and a nail.

These minor housekeeping annoyances (aka, avoidances) are what I
affectionately call "tolerations." They have been ignored for so long that
we forget we have them. The doors stay ajar, the windows get propped
open with sticks, the art remains unhung, and we walk around it.

We adjust. We make do. We deal.

Tolerations are not just irritations that get ignored. On a deeper level
they represent stuck energy. Addressing the issue releases the energy.
Pretty simple, really.

Going away for six months on sabbatical gave us a chance to see our
cute and quirky house with new eyes. One quick call to a handyman,

and we finally got our doors to close properly and our windows to open. It took us, what, twenty years to make that call?!

A-may-zing [angels singing here]! And what is even more amazing is that the shift is palpable.

What is a task you've been avoiding?

Explore

- One task that I've been avoiding is . . .
- The holding pattern feels like . . .
- Allowing and being with my resistance feels like . . .

DAY 30
TOLERATIONS

Tolerations become the background noise of our life: the frayed bedspread, the box of photos that need sorting, the dirty windows, the squeaky cabinet door, the chipped teapot, the missing buttons, the dripping faucet, the slow-draining sink . . . Can you feel the stuckness in these words?

Tolerations are also those clearing projects we haven't yet addressed, like taking things to Goodwill, having a yard sale, or calling someone to take away the junk in the garage. Tolerations keep us stuck in a rut and prevent energy from moving more freely.

Addressing one toleration every day is a surefire way to create momentum, raise the energy, and feel really good! It's also a perfect thing to do when you only have a short bit of time on your hands. Tomorrow you will have a chance to compile a list of your tolerations.

Today do a scan of your home and simply notice. Notice the things that bug you. Notice *how you feel* about the things that bug you. Notice your self-judgments around the things that bug you.

Explore

- The things that bug me are . . .

- This is how they make me feel . . . (Go for it here, with all six senses.)

- I am judging myself for not addressing these issues in these ways . . .

DAY 31
MAKE A LIST OF TOLERATIONS

From yesterday's home scan, compile a list of all the tolerations that need to be addressed.

Once complete, go through your list and give each line item a number between 1 and 10, where 1 represents a quick fix or high-priority task and 10 represents a longer, multistep process.

Here's an **example list**:

- Replace light bulb—1 (easy)

- Replace mildewed shower curtain—3 (two steps: buy the curtain first, then install it)

- Hand wash wool sweaters—5 (not a high priority)

- Clear bulletin board—7 (overwhelming quantity of expired flyers, coupons, faded photos, useless phone numbers; this will take time)

- Tighten screw on shower handle—1 (easy)

- Downsize extra food storage containers—7 (big resistance over this one)

- Declutter email inbox—8 (swimming in emails; this will take time)

- Back up computer—1 (way overdue)
- Refinance the house—10 (multistep process)

To gain momentum and experience immediate energy shifts, high-light the tolerations in the 1–5 category to be addressed first. Begin with the 1s and continue to chip away until the list is complete.

Place tolerations in the higher categories (those that require more time or multiple steps) on a separate list, and if possible break each down into smaller, manageable to-dos. Creating a living will, for example, might have sub–line items such as "ask around for names of good attorneys," "call lawyer to set up appointment," and "talk to relatives."

Once you've compiled your master list, address at least one task per week, beginning with the easier ones (this will keep you from falling into catatonic despair).

Explore
- My tolerations are teaching me the following about myself . . .
- The first toleration(s) I will address will be . . .

DAY 32
SWEEP TO MOVE STUCK ENERGY

There is another simple way to move stuck energy. It's called the kitchen broom.

Whenever I feel stuck in my head or I can't find a solution to a problem that I'm noodling on, or my kitchen floor is just plain dirty, it helps to sweep the floor.

The ordinary act of sweeping is one of the quickest ways I know to energize your life and get centered. Add awareness to this ordinary household activity, and it can also soothe the nervous system, bring you into a meditative state, and just plain make you feel better.

Sometime today, pick up a broom and sweep one small area of your home. Notice how it feels to sweep with intention.

Explore
- When I sweep with intention, I notice . . .
- Sweeping helps me quiet the mind because . . .

DAY 33
CLEARING IS AN INSIDE JOB

In case it hasn't yet sunk in, here's a simple truth about this clearing journey: Clearing is an inside job that begins and ends with you. When you clear the clutter on the inside, the clutter on the outside takes care of itself.

What changes have you noticed in your life from adopting a slower, gentler, and more mindful approach to clearing what holds you back?

Explore
- Some of the changes I've noticed in my life from slowing down and being more mindful are . . .
- I know that clearing starts with me because . . .

DAY 34
RAISE THE ENERGY

You know that feeling when you're so happy you could almost explode? That feeling of being in the right place at the right time, where synchronicities abound, and all is right with the world?

That feeling is real. It's alive. It is you.

Elizabeth Barrett Browning wrote about this feeling in her poem "Aurora Leigh" back in 1856—she said "Earth's crammed with heaven." What is one thing you could do today to gain just a slice of this heaven? What action could you pursue with exuberance?

One thing you might try is listening to certain types of music to change your mood. I find that listening to hot salsa, Latin jazz, or any song by Earth, Wind & Fire when I'm working out at the gym is almost guaranteed to lift my energy level and spirits.

Do one thing today to improve your mood, and watch how your change in energy affects everything.

Explore

- Some surefire ways to raise my energy level and get me going are . . .
- One thing I can do to lift my energy right now is . . . (If you notice any resistance, lean into it.)

DAY 35
CHECK IN—MOVING STUCK ENERGY

This week we played with releasing stuck energy by addressing tolerations, sweeping intentionally, and raising our level of joy. Lifting our spirits and lightening our load begins and ends with us.

Did you notice the energy lifting or shifting this week when you addressed a specific task? What was your biggest aha moment this week?

Explore

- Stuck energy shows up in my life in these ways . . .
- I know that I'm releasing stuck energy when . . .
- My biggest aha moment this week was . . .

WEEK 6
TUNING UP
THE SENSES

Memories establish the past;
Senses perceive the present;
Imaginations shape the future.
　　　　—Toba Beta, *My Ancestor Was an Ancient Astronaut*

DAY 36
SMELL

I can smell things a mile away—people smoking in their cars with the windows rolled up; bread baking down the block; even an opportunity or a scam.

Having a good schnoz is a wonderful quality to have when you're walking through a flower market, or bathing with a brand-new bar of lavender soap. It is divinely transporting. But this gift can also be an occupational hazard if you're trained, as I am, to tune in to the energy in a disturbed space.

What keeps me sane as a highly sensitive person living in a highly sensory world is that I don't identify with every "stinky" or strange sensation that I encounter.

Can you pay attention to smells that are both pleasant and unpleasant without judging them? Try it: Take a deep whiff of your morning coffee, or make a meal that delivers a heavenly aroma. Smell a closet. Smell the earth. Step into the aromatic experience like a curious detective on a data gathering mission.

What does your sense of smell reveal about you, others, or certain spaces? Do you notice the intensity of a smell changing when you simply witness it?

Explore

- My sense of smell is teaching me . . .
- When I bring my full awareness to a specific or intense smell, I notice . . .

DAY 37
TASTE

Tasting is one of life's greatest pleasures. Nature offers up a cornucopia of tastes and flavors—sweet, sour, umami, salty, bitter. And as with smells, not every taste is mouth-watering. There are experiences that can leave a bad taste in your mouth. Whatever the experience, our sense of taste can deliver valuable information.

When I'm space clearing people's homes, for example, I might notice a taste in my mouth that wasn't there before. Dry mouth, for instance, lets me know that I'm processing a disturbance in the environment. A sudden metallic taste is an indicator for me of electromagnetic energies. A medicinal taste clues me in that someone in the home has been sick, or there is a signature of sickness left by a previous occupant that has not been cleared. Because I don't identify these sensations as mine, none ever last long.

Use today to practice tuning in to and exploring your sense of taste. Try foods that you normally don't reach for. Look for subtleties. Notice if certain spaces generate more saliva or dry you out.

Practice just observing with this exercise; allow, and do not identify. Notice if paying exquisite attention to a particular taste changes your experience of it.

Explore

- I'm learning these things about taste . . .
- When I'm in different spaces, I notice these things going on in my mouth . . .

DAY 38
TOUCH

If you're a kinesthetic person, it means that you tend to lead with your sense of touch. You feel your way through a problem and its solution. You love to touch things, read textures using your hands. Bodyworkers and hands-on healers are masters at letting their hands do the talking.

Hands have a divine intelligence. They know where to go where they are needed the most. If you've ever noticed your hand laying on your belly when it's upset, or on your heart when you're in pain, that would be your body's wisdom at work.

Your practice today is to tune in to your sense of touch. Reach for fabrics, textures, weights, and feel them with awareness. Notice your impulse to touch someone who is hurting. Notice the vulnerabilities and fears that may arise at the thought of touching someone or being touched. Place your hand over your heart for a moment and notice what happens to your state of being.

Explore

- I'm learning these things about touch . . .
- When I place my hand on a body part that is contracted or in pain, I feel . . .

DAY 39
HEAR

If you're an auditory person, you'll hear things most people don't. My husband is auditory. He can't help but hear what's being said when someone walks by while they're talking on their cell, and he'll pick up on conversations of those sitting nearby at a packed restaurant. He processes words and sounds like a human antenna, not because he's snoopy, but because he's wired that way. I can be sitting at the same table and not hear a thing.

Where I get snagged is with loud noises. Any sudden or repetitive sound, such as a car alarm, will make me recoil. Heavy metal music is a full-body assault and plain hurts.

Are there certain sounds that you are drawn to over others? How sensitive is your hearing? How selective is your listening?

Today's practice is to tune in with all ears. Pay attention to the ambient sounds around you, noticing which sounds are calming and which ones feel uncomfortable. For contrast, turn on the radio and listen to music that is calming for a minute, then switch the channel to a station that plays loud, jarring music. Notice the effects of each on your mind and nervous system.

If you cannot avoid certain unpleasant sounds in your life, look for ways to help you selectively listen, such as practicing mindfulness, yoga, and meditation.

Explore
- I'm learning these things about sound . . .
- These sounds please me . . .
- These sounds hurt my ears . . .

DAY 40
SEE

Have you ever looked for something that was hiding in plain sight? Like losing your reading glasses only to find them literally on top of your nose? Or discovering the missing carton of milk was on the top shelf of the fridge all along?

Seeing is all about perception. The mind has a funny way of showing us exactly what we want to see and can handle.

Seeing is also a function of how clear we are in our home, head, and heart. Just like a window that has been cleaned, it's amazing how much more gets revealed through both our physical eyes and our mind's eye when we are clear.

It was Georgia O'Keeffe who once said, "To see takes time." What do you want to see? What are you afraid to see?

Try it: Look around you and allow your eyes to rest on one thing. Take a minute to examine and study it. If it's the crumbs of toast that were left on the breakfast table, for example, notice their shape and how they landed, without judging the mess. Gaze at a flower that's just about to bloom. Look at people's faces on the subway. Study a photograph one day, and repeat the action the next day. Do you see something there you hadn't noticed before?

Do it for no other purpose than to grow your seeing muscle.

Explore
- I'm learning these things about seeing . . .
- I want to see . . .
- I'm afraid to see . . .

DAY 41
INTUIT

We cannot talk about sensing without including the sixth sense. Call it divine intuition, inner knowing, your gut instinct. It can be that voice telling you to do or not do something, or that something is about to happen in your life. It is a deep knowing without proof to back it up.

It was my sixth sense that told me a house my husband and I were about to buy years ago wasn't meant to be. The day before signing the papers with the seller, I was at the house measuring the windows for curtains. Out of nowhere I got a very clear voice that said to me: *Don't bother measuring, Stephanie. You will not be living here.* The inner voice was accompanied by a visual image of four large windows. These were not the windows I had been measuring. I had no idea where they were.

I didn't want to hear that voice, of course, and I pushed it away. I didn't even tell my husband about this "crazy thinking." We loved the house and were giddy to buy after waiting so long to find it.

Then, lo and behold, the seller bailed on us. We watched in disbelief as she held the document in her hands with a pen pointed at the signature line. She couldn't do it. We were devastated.

Fast-forward six weeks. We found another house—an even better one than the first! There, in the front room, were the four windows I had seen in my head.

As I like to say, it pays to follow your "knows." There is a lot less suffering.

Explore
- The last time I remember having an intuitive insight was . . .
- When I know something for sure, I feel . . .

DAY 42
CHECK IN—TUNING UP THE SENSES

The focus this week was on refining and deepening our senses—smell, taste, touch, hearing, seeing, and inner knowing. As human "doers" living mostly on autopilot, we neglect to tap the intelligence that comes through the body. Together, the six senses are the processing center of clearing. Without conscious sensing, there is no clearing. Period.

Have you been able to identify which of your sense(s) you tend to use the most when relating to things, people, or spaces? Do you notice that some people and spaces feel differently than others? Do you notice yourself being drawn to certain sights and sounds and recoiling from others?

Explore

- The sense(s) I tend to use most that I now recognize as a gift are . . .
- Something new I learned about myself after a week of conscious sensing is . . .

WEEK 7
EMBRACING EMOTIONAL WEATHER

You are the sky. Everything else—it's just the weather.
—Pema Chödrön

DAY 43
~~SPRING~~ YEAR-ROUND CLEARING

Why is it that every spring when we crawl out of our winter caves, we go into a wild frenzy of clearing the chaos that has snuck its way back into our homes and lives? It's like somewhere around mid-fall we lost our way, forgot all our good intentions from the previous spring, and find ourselves scrambling again at square one.

As I see it, spring clearing has nothing to do with spring or cleaning.

Clearing our spaces is a journey that starts right where we are. It makes no difference if the spaces are the external ones in which we live and work, or the internal ones that we fill up with a chattering, worrying mind.

All you need to get the energy moving in your home and life is to clear something. A toothpick, a paper clip, a measly crumb. Anything will do so long as you clear it with compassionate awareness—every day.

Just as a butterfly's wings in one part of the world can create massive weather changes in another, baby steps can lead to a sea change in your life—a clearing movement of global proportions.

Explore

- Three things that move me out of stuckness are . . .
- One small thing I can do today to start my clearing movement is . . .

DAY 44
IT'S ONLY WEATHER

Weather is a perfect metaphor to describe everything that we are *not*. It is also a terrific tool to help us cultivate detachment.

In a way, our emotions are no different than the weather: We can be flattened by an emotional squall, feel lost under a blanket of fog, throw a tantrum with lightning ferocity. No matter what our low pressure system looks like, it is a state of being that is guaranteed to shift (and lift) when we don't make it ours.

Today, when you feel a twinge of worry, fear, sadness, attachment, or any sensation that points to a resisting weather pattern, take a deep breath and repeat this mantra out loud to yourself: It's only weather.

And watch what happens.

Explore

- When I reframe my state of being with "It's only weather," this is what happens . . .
- I know that "weather" of any kind is not mine because . . .

DAY 45
WEATHER WATCH

Maria Montessori has a wonderful saying that sums up her approach to education perfectly: "We cannot create observers by saying 'observe' . . .

these means are procured through education of the senses." In that spirit, I'd like to invite you to use today to witness the weather patterns in your life—both the low pressure systems and the high pressure ones—using your six senses. Notice a lingering sadness, an impatient outburst, a wave of shame, a foggy mind. Notice if there are certain times of day when you are more likely to feel "under the weather."

Carry this practice into the rest of your day: Watch your internal weather system moving in and out, in and out, like breathing.

Explore

- I'm learning these things about the weather patterns in my life . . .
- When I simply observe, I notice these changes in myself . . .

DAY 46
UNDER THE WEATHER

It took me years to learn why I felt so yucky every time I cleared a drawer or a closet.

Sorting through a pile of books, for example, always made me feel congested, gummy, and thirsty. My head would feel cobwebby (just like the books), and my feet would always ache after an hour of moving things around. And the less certain I was about letting something go, the more foggy-headed I felt.

It wasn't until I was studying space clearing that I learned why. It's because clutter is a sticky, dense energy. The longer we have it, the denser and stickier it gets.

As you begin to consciously clear the stress and the stuff you've been holding on to, the body responds and processes the changes—not unlike the stormy weather that gets stirred when a high pressure system collides with a low pressure one. It's like you're detoxifying your home (and yourself), which doesn't always feel very good.

Is just reading these words enough to elicit a bodily response? If you're noticing a drag on your energy level, or unexplainable yuckiness that wasn't there before, that is because ideas—as energy—can affect us just like anything else.

Name and feel the sensations (which are not yours, remember?) and let them go. Then follow up by doing something that feels really good to shift the energy.

Explore

- Reading this lesson makes me feel . . .

- One thing I can do to shift my energy is . . .

DAY 47
NAME AND FEEL

In yesterday's lesson, we explored how unconscious discomfort can be a sign of stuck energy. When we bring awareness to the discomfort, we reverse the process and release the stuckness. We may not feel very good right away, but naming and feeling the disturbing effects changes the dynamic completely.

Name and feel the overwhelm. Name and feel the frustration. Name and feel the blame and shame. That is the work.

Even if you have no words to name something, you can feel it by bringing all six of your senses to bear—with awareness.

What can you name and feel right now? Can you name and feel your emotional weather without judging the experience, or yourself? (If you could use a little refresher on how to do this, I invite you to revisit the Feeling Check process from Day 20.)

Explore

- One thing that is bothering me today is . . .
- This thing makes me feel . . . (Notice any judgments creeping up.)

DAY 48
TREAT YOURSELF

It may not look like much on paper, but naming and feeling weather patterns is big bioenergetic work. Releasing a lifetime of stuck patterns is the best, and sometimes the hardest, work you'll ever do. And if your journey takes you through some thick, foggy patches to process old stuff—as it has for me so many times—you may not realize how wiped out you are.

It's for this reason that I invite you to take some time today to rest. Treat yourself to some nourishing self-care—a walk, a cup of tea, a hot bath—anything that moves you to feel good, held, comforted.

Yes, you *always* have permission to rest.

Explore

- One thing I can do today to nourish myself and rest is . . . (Notice the impulse to press on; name and feel the resistance to taking time for yourself.)
- I must take time to integrate big changes because . . .

DAY 49
CHECK IN—EMBRACING EMOTIONAL WEATHER

This week we played with the concept of weather to describe any symptom of imbalance that clouds who we are. We lift and release weather patterns by naming and feeling our discomfort. This includes taking time to integrate and rest afterward.

What have you observed about your unique weather system? What has helped to soften and clear it? Did you notice any shifting and lifting of sensations? For example, perhaps you noticed that a throbbing headache dissolved simply because you watched it with curious or spacious detachment.

Explore
- Weather shows up in my life in these ways . . .
- I know that I'm releasing weather when . . .
- When I clear without judging myself, I notice . . .

WEEK 8
SLOWING DOWN

For fast-acting relief, try slowing down.
—Lily Tomlin

DAY 50
LIFE IN THE SLOW LANE

Last year, my husband and I left our home in Massachusetts to spend six months in Mexico. We rented out our home, uploaded books on tape, got in the car, and drove 3,000 miles to our home south of the border—a place where we could unplug from life as usual.

And what a big reveal it was! From boot camp opportunities in letting go to mind-bending encounters with nature, beauty, and art, the days were as diverse and varied as the cloud formations at sunset.

Some days, we didn't have Internet or electricity, and those alternatively seemed to go on forever while others passed in the blink of an eye. Such is life in the slow lane.

If you think you have to move away or have your mind bent in a million different ways to dial it down, think again. If you can find a way to slow down just a little, to simplify your life and allow the queasy discomfort of not knowing what's going to happen next, I would wager that you too would have some pretty jaw-dropping experiences of your own.

What would it mean to you if your life slowed down? Notice the fears or the flutters of excitement as you consider the prospect of dialing down your life.

Explore

- If I dialed down my life a notch or two, it would mean . . .
- This is how things would change for me . . .

DAY 51
FIGHT-OR-FLIGHT

If I've learned anything over the years of clearing, it would be this: Small efforts applied consistently over time are the real game changer.

Slowing down isn't just a good idea that I adopted from years of personal experience. There is plenty of science to back me up. One of the key players in this clearing business is an ancient almond-shape region in the brain called the amygdala. It is our built-in secret service agent, if you will, designed to spring into action the moment it senses danger. (Read: A lion is charging you, or your toddler is reaching for the kitchen knife.) Once the alarm has been triggered, the amygdala shuts down all nonessential functions and sends a cascade of stress hormones throughout the body to heighten and manage the emergency. This is your fight-or-flight response.

The problem with having stress hormones flooding the system is that they won't stop until *you* stop (the negative self-talk, the worry, the recycling of painful memories, etc.).

There is no question that having this defense when you're under real attack is super awesome. It's a big liability, however, when you're up to your eyeballs clearing the nightmare of junk in your closet or basement—stuff that can only be addressed effectively when you feel calm. And safe.

Today, try noticing when your fight-or-flight response kicks in unnecessarily.

Explore
- I know my stress response has been activated when . . .
- I can remember to dial it back by . . .

DAY 52
BABY STEPS

There is a wonderful book by psychologist Dr. Robert Maurer called *One Small Step Can Change Your Life: The Kaizen Way*. In it, he makes a compelling case for dialing down our efforts:

> Small, easily achievable goals—such as picking up and storing just one paper clip on a chronically messy desk—let you tiptoe right past the amygdala, keeping it asleep and unable to set off alarm bells. As your small steps continue and your cortex starts working, the brain begins to create "software" for your desired change, actually laying down new nerve pathways and building new habits.

Take a few minutes today to make a list of things or issues that you'd like to release. Choose thoughts, relationships, or situations that elicit a stress response or make you feel uneasy when you think of them. Assign each item a number from 1 to 10, with 1 indicating the least challenging situation and 10 indicating the most challenging.

Notice the sensations that arise as you review your list without judgment. What is one thing from your list of lower numbers that you can handle and release today? Choose something that will not overwhelm you or trigger alarm bells in the brain.

Explore
- One item that I can easily address and release today is . . .
- Dialing it back a notch feels . . .

DAY 53
YOUR INDICATOR TO DIAL IT DOWN

Thich Nhat Hanh tells us, "When you feel overwhelmed, you're trying too hard." How does it feel when you've realized you've taken on more than you can handle? Unleashing a host of stress chemicals is not going to serve you. In fact, it will stop you cold every time.

Next time you hit the proverbial wall, use it as an opportunity to name and feel the frustration, and dial it down. Adopt a gentler "Reduce and Repeat" (R&R) approach: **reduce** the task (or time spent) and **repeat** it until it no longer elicits a stress response.

Take a little time today to revisit yesterday's issues with a high challenge number. Add to your list any additional items that remain, for now, off limits. If it helps, write these down in red ink.

Bookmark this page to come back to later in the year and see if the emotional charge around any of these issues has reduced or disappeared altogether. You may just notice that the clearing magically happens all by itself—something you wouldn't even remember if you hadn't written it down (*wink*).

Explore
- Issues that scare me that I know I need to address someday in the future are . . .
- I should back away from these issues at this time because . . .

DAY 54
THE RULE OF ONE

A good rule of thumb for clearing *anything* is the "rule of one." This helps to calm the mind when you're caught in fight-or-flight.

Here's how it works: Clear one thing (pile, thought, issue) with awareness for one minute, once a day, for one week. Increase the task or time spent by increments of one as you begin to feel more comfortable and safe.

Use today to revisit your ongoing list of things and issues you'd like to release in your home and life. Revise the challenge numbers you've assigned to certain tasks and issues if they seem easier or harder to accomplish after reflection.

Choose one task from your list and see if you can break it down into smaller, more doable tasks, and assign each a challenge number. For example, clearing out the refrigerator, which might have gotten an 8 on your original list, may still give you heart palpitations. If you break down the task into various sub-tasks that would each only elicit a 2 on your challenge meter—like cleaning out one shelf every day, consolidating the condiments, or removing one unidentifiable freezer item—you may find that the refrigerator gets cleared in no time!

Easy peasy.

Explore

- One bigger clearing task I can break down into smaller, one minute tasks is . . .
- One easy thing I can clear for one minute a day every day this week is . . .

DAY 55
TO DO OR NOT TO DO?

While most everyone seems to find my baby-step approach to clearing refreshing and energizing, not everyone is sold. Occasionally I'll receive a comment from a student who is mystified by my counterintuitive invitations to dial it down. So if you too are feeling like nothing is happening yet, or you're wishing you were getting more concrete tips on clearing your house, it might help to remember that this is not a traditional how-to book. The approach here is more about "how to *not* do" in order to allow the emotional stuckness and resisting patterns (that are encoded in the clutter) to soften, bubble up, and release.

For us to break old habits and rewire new ones in ways that are sustainable, we need to practice not engaging the part of the mind that goes into fight-or-flight. Clearing is a daily practice that starts where you are.

Where do you want to start?

Explore
- Going slow is frustrating for me because . . .
- The best place for me to start right now is . . .

DAY 56
CHECK IN—SLOWING DOWN

The focus this week was to practice slowing down by reducing clearing tasks to baby steps so as not to trigger the stress response. Though this approach may be frustrating to a mind conditioned to speed and visible progress, it is more effective and sustainable in the long run. Dialing down creates new neural pathways in the brain that lead to greater traction and well-being.

What new insights have you received from slowing down? For example, did a one-minute clearing effort morph into more minutes spent without your even noticing the passage of time? Did your list of things you'd like to release increase or reduce your sense of anxiety and overwhelm?

Explore
- What I'm learning about going slow is . . .
- What gets in the way of my slowing down is . . .
- If I could slow down right now, I would . . .

WEEK 9
RELEASING OLD STORIES

The past has served its purpose.
—Panache Desai

DAY 57
SPIN CYCLE

"Spin" works well to describe what we do with thoughts, beliefs, and stories that no longer serve us. It also has a nice double meaning: We can spin a web of worries (untruths, painful memories) like a spider spins her web, or we can chew on a thought so much that we spin in circles and get dizzy—going nowhere fast.

One worry I've been spinning a lot lately concerns knee pain. If I really reflect on it, my mind can sound a bit morose and harpy: *No matter how hard I try—all the yoga I do, all the supplements I take, and all the physical therapy I pay for—my knees are a wreck. I feel like an old lady hobbling down the stairs . . .*

None of these refrains are going to help me heal, of course. That's just the mind on autopilot when it's unhappy. When I'm not too lost in the story and can remember to choose differently, I'll reach for my tried-and-true antidotes—positive reframes that I breathe into, like these: "I step forward fluidly and deliberately"; "I glide with grace and ease"; "I am doing everything to bring greater flexibility to my knees and heal . . ."

The phrasing is important. Notice that I use words that are evocative and palpable; words that help me feel *how I want to feel.*

What is one worry or negative belief that you spin a lot that you could reframe? Once you have it, breathe it in like manna from heaven.

Explore

- One worry or negative belief that I spin a lot is . . .
- I can rephrase it in a way that feels really good by . . .

DAY 58
REDUCE THE CHARGE, RELEASE THE STORY

War: bad. Control-freak boss: bad. Snow: bad for traffic (good for the drought).

It's okay to have an opinion. Where it gets messy is when the opinion holds a lot of charge; i.e., it magnetizes more distress and fear and makes it harder for us to be "bigger than" the story.

Thoughts and emotions that carry a strong negative charge have a way of pulling us in and holding us hostage. (This is a big reason why practicing awareness and extreme self-care is so important in our clearing work.) Here's one of many painful examples of how negative charge (anger, in this case) can escalate and gobble us up. In the case of this brave student, Marti S., it took a health crisis for her to awaken and redirect the course of her life:

My ex [husband] fathered a child with a much younger woman years ago. The shock almost did me in, but the anger was so palpable that I ate and slept with it daily . . . until, six months later, I got breast cancer. It hit me that it wasn't the cancer that would kill me, but my anger. I'm not saying "forgive" with a big F. . . . All I'm sharing is to HEAL YOU daily. Love your reason for being on this earth now, which is not about him. It's about being free now to choose your own cool destiny ahead.

What "bad" stories are you spinning today? What is one thing you can do to reduce the negative charge?

You are not your story.

Explore
- A story I'm spinning (telling myself) today is . . .
- One way I can reduce the charge I'm holding around it is . . .
- I know I'm not my story because . . .

DAY 59
UNLOAD THE FAMILY BAGGAGE

The thing about unconscious belief patterns and negative emotions is that they don't exist in isolation. Energetically they create a sticky field that attracts more negative thoughts and emotions. The stronger the charge, and the longer they've been around, the stickier their effects can be on our psyche, relationships, and living spaces. Until the negative charge is released, any stuck patterns and unconscious human behaviors will continue to morph, expand, and repeat themselves.

This is especially true of thoughts and emotions that have been passed down from generation to generation, as shared so beautifully by my online student Elle N. here:

Tonight I randomly came across the movie *The Joy Luck Club*, a beautiful story of female pain and joy intertwined across generations of mother–daughter relationships and family history, and it helped me understand a great deal of what is holding me back.

Generational clutter, generational chaos, generational pain. We hold so much of our family baggage, and there have been studies showing that this is passed down through DNA. When you consider how heavy this must become through the years, it's no wonder we often can't separate our stories from those we have carried subconsciously. Tonight I cried the tears of my broken heart for all that my family could not give to me and that which they did—both good and bad. Tomorrow I am allowing myself to be present and to begin exploring and unpacking that which is mine and to repackage and return to sender that which is not.

What stories and beliefs have you been carrying for your family that you are now ready to release?

It may help to know that lightening your energetic load with compassionate awareness creates a powerful ripple effect: It lightens the load for everyone who came before you and will come after.

Explore

- Some stories and beliefs from family that I'm now ready to release are . . .
- Naming and letting go of what is not mine feels . . .
- Knowing that lightening my load lightens the load of everyone in my family line makes me feel . . .

DAY 60
IT IS SAFE TO LET THIS GO

"It is safe for me to let this go" is a deceptively powerful statement and easy enough to say. But how easy is it to *believe*? How easy is it to repeat it in the face of the stories you tell yourself?

Maybe not so easy at first. It might bring up some disbelief and discomfort.

Keep swirling the phrase around your consciousness over time, though, and you may just notice how it frees some false debris . . . little by little . . . like flecks of peeling paint that reveal the sparkly truth of who you are.

Explore

- A story I tell myself (that I know is not true) that I'd like to release is . . .
- It is safe for me to let go of this story because . . . (Notice and allow the part of you that does not feel so safe.)

DAY 61
SIMPLE CLEARING PROCESS

Is there a worry you've been spinning that you would like to clear? Perhaps it's a sick family member, financial strain, or a future that does not look so bright at the moment. No matter how big or how small the issue, call it up with as much detail as you can and use the short **all-purpose visualization** that follows to help release it.

In this process you will be asked to tune in to your personal energy field. This is the invisible, subtle energy field that radiates out from the physical body like the growth rings of a tree. You do not need to believe in its existence for this process to work its magic.

1. **Close your eyes**, and take an easy breath in and out. Do a full-body feeling check (like the one you did on Day 20), noticing and allowing all sensations.
2. **Notice** your breathing. Is it shallow? Is it full?
3. When you feel centered, **recall** a worry that you've been carrying with as much detail as you can. Imagine the worry

as a ball of sticky, sluggish energy swirling in your personal energy field.

4. With as much compassionate awareness as you can, **imagine** this mass getting smaller and smaller, losing its grip, and finally dissolving.

5. When you feel complete, **invite** a sparkling, golden light energy to fill you up: to infuse, refresh, and restore you completely.

6. **Open your eyes** when you're ready and notice how you feel.

Repeat this simple clearing process every day this week until the sticky energy has lifted.

Explore

- One thing that has been worrying me a lot lately is . . .
- Before the meditation I was feeling . . .
- Now I feel . . .

DAY 62
IT'S NOT ABOUT YOU

This message came to me fully formed in a dream: "The work is not about you. It's about clearing the 'you' you *think* is you so that you can fully access and realize the one that has been there all along."

You'll probably have to read that one again. Even I had to process this message for it to fully sink in.

What is wanting to reveal itself to you, and in what ways do you hold yourself back from experiencing it?

Explore
- What is wanting to reveal itself to me is . . .
- Ways I hold back . . .

DAY 63
CHECK IN—RELEASING OLD STORIES

Stories are what we tell ourselves. They are not who we are. The focus this week was to look at some of the thoughts and beliefs we spin that no longer serve and support us, and to apply simple clearing practices to reduce their emotional impact. By naming and feeling our personal pain with compassionate awareness, we can release the negative charge that these stories hold, stop their spinning, and heal what has been passed unconsciously from generation to generation.

Why is it safe to let these stories go? Do you feel differently today than you did a week ago? How so?

Explore
- It's safe to let my stories go because . . .
- I feel differently now than I did a week ago in these ways . . .

WEEK 10
PARING DOWN
THE PURSE

I reached between the seats to the backseat, where her purse was on the floor. It was the size of a grocery bag and it weighed a ton.

"What the hell do you have in this thing?"

"Everything."

—Michael Connelly, *The Gods of Guilt*

DAY 64
THE MIGHTY PURSE

I was with my dear friend Meg one evening when her husband offered to put her "purse" (read: bag the size of a small suitcase) in the car so that she wouldn't have to lug it around.

Spilling out of that thing was a tangle of earphones, a massive keychain with a metal ornament that weighed about ten pounds, and who knows what else. It was so full of stuff she struggled to zip it closed. I watched her clutch that thing even closer when her husband asked again. I could see by her squinting eyes that giving up this precious cargo was going to take some time. *I can't go anywhere without my purse! What if I need . . .*

None of it is conscious, of course.

Yes, she wanted to carry it. So habituated to the tether, it had never occurred to her that she had a choice.

After some lighthearted ribbing and a quick tour of the minimal handbag I was carrying, my friend realized that it was safe to go native.

Is there anything in your purse (wallet, backpack) that doesn't need to be there?

If so, here's your chance to remove it. With awareness.

Explore
- The thought of clearing out my bag makes me feel . . .
- If I were to guess, my everyday bag weighs about . . .

DAY 65
DECONSTRUCTING THE PURSE—PART 1

I emailed my friend with the mammoth bag a few days later to tell her that I was going to do a segment in my book on handbags, and I wondered if she cared to weigh in (as it were). I was curious to know, specifically, what she might consider "nonessential."

Here's Meg H.'s thoughtful reply:

I consider everything in there to be essential. I guess the trick is that it's not all essential ALL THE TIME, so your idea of having smaller purses for different things (not just different events) is a great one. Kind of like little submarines that siphon stuff from the mother ship. So, for example, I have all my various cards (bookstore, Starbucks, insurance, whatever) that form a thick wad. The change I carry around is surprisingly heavy. This is stuff I could leave behind a lot of the time, but not ALL the time, and that's the key—to take a minute before I go out to ask myself just what I need to carry for that outing. Problem is, this takes time, and it's easier just to grab the bag. It's a conundrum.

This is one of those daily nagging items! Reminds me of what former Texas governor Ann Richards told legislators when she vetoed a concealed carry bill after they said that concealed carry would make it easier for ladies to carry guns in their bags to protect themselves: "Honey, everybody knows that no woman can find a damn thing in her purse!"

How is your current handbag working for you (or not)? What do you consider the ideal handbag?

Explore
- My current handbag works for me (doesn't work for me) because . . .
- The ideal handbag would be . . .

DAY 66
DECONSTRUCTING THE PURSE—PART 2

You do not need to carry everything around with you everywhere you go.

Let me say that again. *You do not need to carry everything around with you everywhere you go.*

And yes, it will take some time and concentration to decide what stays and what goes.

I'm a hands-free kind of gal when it comes to handbags. I am also partial to purses with lots of zippers that I can carry around my shoulder or on my back. I hate rooting around for things, so I keep a maximum of three to four things in each zippered compartment.

During the day I'll carry a larger backpack-style purse. In the front pocket I keep my car keys, cell phone, reading glasses, and lipstick. In the back zippered compartment (hidden from view) I keep my wallet. In the middle compartment I store things I don't need to reach for as often: a notebook, pen, sunglasses, comb. The thing weighs about one pound total.

For evening outings, I'll switch to a very small purse that I can carry around my shoulder with only the absolute essentials: reading glasses, cell phone, lipstick, driver's license, and one credit card. My nighttime purse is practically weightless.

If I need an extra coat, umbrella, or bottle of water, I'll use a large shoulder bag that I can leave in the car or put under a chair. I'll put small bags inside bigger ones like Russian dolls so that I can easily see what I have and consolidate.

In preparation for tomorrow's pruning, your task today is to take inventory of your bag using the three prompts that follow.

Explore
- The items currently in my handbag are . . . (Naming and feeling the overwhelm, the shame, and/or the squirmy resistance is key to this process.)
- The items I cannot leave home without are . . .
- Taking inventory of my bag feels . . .

DAY 67
STAY, GO, THROW, DON'T KNOW

One of my favorite workshops is when I invite everyone in the room to grab his or her purse, wallet, or backpack and dump the entire contents on the floor. You can imagine the eye rolls, groans, and squeals that fill the room as everyone comes face-to-face with the pleasant and not-so-pleasant reveals.

Once the cat is out of the bag, participants are asked to group the contents into four piles:

1. **Stay**—The Stay pile comprises all the essentials that must travel with you: wallet, credit cards, driver's license, cell phone, house keys, reading glasses, medications.

2. **Go**—The Go pile is for the hitchhikers: those things that do not belong in your purse and are not essential to your survival and well-being.

3. **Throw**—The Throw pile is for things like old ticket stubs, candy wrappers—anything that can be tossed or recycled.

4. **Don't Know**—The Don't Know pile is for everything else that you're not sure what to do with. Set this pile aside and deal with it after you've addressed the first three.

Your task today is to clear your purse, backpack, or backseat of your car—whatever could use some pruning today—following the four-pile method above. If it's too much to handle an entire purse or backpack, dial it down. Clear just *one* compartment, and repeat the same process the next day, or until complete.

Explore
- Paring down my purse (wallet, backpack) feels . . .
- Resistances I feel when I come face to face with it are . . .

DAY 68
CONSCIOUS PRUNING

Here's what I'm wondering: Did you happen to add awareness to yesterday's clearing?

That was just a taster. Here's what the same practice would look like if you added compassionate awareness. Try it again with the same item that you cleared yesterday (or choose a different object that could use some attention), and clear it using the pruning process that follows:

1. **Empty** *all* the contents of your bag onto a clear surface or the floor.

2. **Group** your belongings into the four piles: Stay, Go, Throw, Don't Know.

3. **Close your eyes**, and take a couple minutes to notice and allow all sensations: How's your breathing? Are you rushing? Are you thirsty? Are you judging yourself? Are you feeling any pangs of embarrassment or shame? What do the pangs feel like, and where in your body do you feel them?

4. **Allow** all sensations to arise without doing anything to fix, change, or manage them.

5. When you feel complete, **open your eyes** and put your things away with awareness beginning with the Stay pile and ending with the Don't Know pile.

6. **Notice** if you're feeling differently from when you started.

7. **Write down** any aha moments in your journal.

In case it hasn't quite sunk in, this exercise is not about fixing a problem. And it's not a race to see how much you can "get done." The practice is designed to slow *you* down so you can allow the resisting patterns to arise, be witnessed with spacious detachment, and released.

The pudgy purse (rat's nest refrigerator, excess body weight, painful relationship, unsatisfying career—or whatever causes you pain) is simply the vehicle that takes your clearing to a much deeper level.

Explore

- Of the four piles, the one that challenges me the most is . . . (and ways that I could reduce its size and impact on me might be . . .)

- When I insert awareness into a clearing exercise (versus just "doing" the exercise) I notice . . .

DAY 69
"I HAVE NO TIME!"

The time thing is a conundrum. Whatever you're clearing or moving around takes time.

Here's the thing: It's not about having no time. It's that we make other things more important. If we turn the task of moving things around into a daily practice that promotes well-being, it will never feel onerous. The more a task feels good, the more we'll *want to take the time* to do it.

In the case of my purse, making strategic transfers from one bag to another takes me one minute. Two, tops. And when I slow down even more (on purpose), and insert awareness, the task actually feels meditative and good. It helps me gather the loose ends of myself and feel better.

What are you making time for that is not useful or nourishing? What could you do instead with that time? What is holding you back?

Explore
- Things I've made time for that are not useful or nourishing are . . .
- I could instead do . . .
- Resistances that come up when I consider making a pivot are . . .

DAY 70
CHECK IN—PARING DOWN THE PURSE

The focus this week was to use that thing we lug around everywhere we go—our handbag, wallet, computer bag, backpack—as a practice tool in letting go. When we make it a priority to slow down, simple practices in sorting, pruning, and moving things around have the added benefit of promoting well-being.

What has your handbag taught you about you? In what ways does inserting awareness into an everyday task feel more nourishing (or less onerous)?

Explore

- My bag has taught me . . .
- Inserting awareness into daily pruning feels . . .

WEEK 11
SENSING ENERGY IN THINGS AND SPACES

There's a reason they built those cathedrals. Pick your place, on purpose.

—Seth Godin, "The Space Matters"

DAY 71
NOT ALL SPACES FEEL THE SAME

Have you noticed that not all spaces feel good—even the brand-new, empty, and clutter-free ones?

Since I was a little girl, long before I knew what space clearing was, I would go into certain homes feeling just fine and come away feeling like I'd been hit over the head with a sledgehammer. My beloved uncle's house, the seaside home of a friend in Maine, some of the centuries-old homes in my childhood neighborhood of Mexico City—all had a similar effect: they made me feel ill or uneasy whenever I stepped into them. Stomachaches, waves of nausea, and even the flu were common side effects. It didn't matter if the space was a jaw-dropping mansion or a spartan studio apartment.

I didn't know what was going on at the time, of course. Nor did I have a means to consciously process and detach from the sensory overload. If there was something funky going on, I would soak up the unsavory energies and take them home with me.

Whose home(s) do you love to visit, and whose do you avoid? Which commercial spaces (warehouse stores, doctors' offices, airport terminals, libraries, city parks, etc.) feel good to you, and which do not?

Notice if your mind is searching for *reasons* for why some spaces feel good while others do not, and why it matters. Use this exercise to simply observe and allow any queasiness that arises.

Explore
- Spaces that feel good to me are . . .
- Spaces that don't feel good are . . .

DAY 72
ENERGY IN THE ROOM

Are you aware of the energy in the room you're sitting in right now?

Are you aware of your breathing?

Are you aware of being aware?

Again, nothing to do but notice, breathe, and allow.

Notice the spaces you go into and out of during the course of your day. Notice the ones that feel good to you. Witness the contracted ones without passing judgment.

Explore
- What I notice about the space I'm sitting in . . .
- The spaces that I have gone into and out of today feel . . .

DAY 73
FIVE SIMPLE TRUTHS ABOUT ENERGY

After years of clearing the energetic equivalent of clutter in people's living spaces and workplaces, here's what I know, distilled into **five simple truths**:

1. We are energy beings.
2. As energy beings, we are connected to everything and everyone. There is no separation.
3. Fear and attachment vibrate at a lower frequency than love and joy.
4. Limiting beliefs and negative emotions can stick to things, people, and spaces.
5. Not everything we feel is ours.

Which of these statements got your attention and why? Spend today seeing everything as a form of vibrating energy: your home, possessions, relationships, coworkers, challenges, guilty pleasures, trees, rocks . . .

Some forms of energy are denser and more sluggish than others. Can you tell the difference?

Explore
- The simple truth that got my attention was . . . (because . . .)
- I'm able to discern energetic differences between . . .

DAY 74
ENERGY IN THINGS

Are you aware of being drawn to certain possessions in your home, and discomfited by others? Things like jewelry, antiques, family heirlooms, photographs, furniture, rugs?

Try it: Choose an object that does not feel good, preferably something old or antique that hasn't been used or looked at in a while. It could be your great grandmother's engagement ring, an old photo album, a set of china teacups.

Take a minute to hang out with this item and allow all sensations to arise without judging them. (*Note:* If you start to feel any intense "weather" moving in, stop the exercise and do something that feels good instead. You'll get to revisit this exercise again tomorrow.)

Explore
- The object that I tuned in to today that doesn't feel good . . .
- Sensations that I noticed when I tuned in to it . . . (Feel the thing, don't analyze it.)

DAY 75
GOOD JUJU, BAD JUJU

Can objects have bad juju? You know, like the beautiful heirloom that doesn't feel quite right? That antique mask you got really cheap at the consignment store that smells funny? The sixteenth-century Chinese chest you saw at the museum that made you feel dizzy? If so, what is the best way to clear these things?

I get questions like these often in my line of work, like this one:

I was given an African fertility figure from a relative many years ago . . . Whether real or imagined, I feel it may have a deep and dark, negative effect for those who touch it. I would like to get rid of it. Throw it out, burn it. How can I get rid of this and be done with it safely? It seems silly, but for some reason I feel compelled to be careful in how I dispose of this piece.

I know the impulse to "get rid of, throw it out, burn it" very well. When we humans are confronted with a situation that scares us, pushes our buttons, or doesn't feel very good, the natural reaction is to contract and flee. That stress response, once unleashed, makes clearing it much harder. Being attached to a particular outcome, or being attached to the belief that there is something "bad" that needs getting rid of, does not restore balance nor bring about lasting change.

This is why I recommend trying a different approach: a daily baby-step approach to clearing that will help calm the fearful mind and reduce the disturbing effects of any thing or issue that plagues you—be it an object like your African fertility figure, a funky corner of the closet, or a challenging relationship that rattles your cage.

Tune in again to the object you worked with yesterday. Do you notice any shifts in how it feels today? Have the sensations subsided, eased, or intensified? Do you notice it looks clearer (more sparkly, less dull)? If this object could talk, what would it say to you?

Explore
- When I tune in to the object that I worked with yesterday I notice . . .
- If this object could talk, it would tell me . . .

DAY 76
THE SPACE MATTERS

At the end of the day, choosing where we spend our time can make all the difference in how productive we are and how good we feel.

In his blog post "The Space Matters," thought leader Seth Godin gives us a good reason to think twice before picking a spot:

It might be a garage or a sunlit atrium, but the place you choose to do what you do has an impact on you.

More people get engaged in Paris in the springtime than on the 7 train in Queens. They just do. Something in the air, I guess.

Pay attention to where you have your brainstorming meetings. Don't have them in the same conference room where you chew people out over missed quarterly earnings.

Pay attention to the noise and the smell and the crowd in the place where you're trying to overcome being stuck . . .

Most of all, I think we can train ourselves to associate certain places with certain outcomes. There's a reason they built those cathedrals. Pick your place, on purpose.

Which spaces serve you best to do what you do? Which do not?

Explore
- I need to spend more time in . . .
- I need to avoid . . . (because . . .)

DAY 77
CHECK IN—SENSING ENERGY IN THINGS AND SPACES

The focus this week was to fine-tune our sensing abilities: to tune in to energetic frequencies of different spaces and objects so that we can become more discerning where we spend our time and with what we choose to surround ourselves.

Were you able to distinguish energies that feel "off" from those that are more sparkly and coherent? What does the impulse to "get rid of" feel like, and what can you do differently when it comes up? In what ways do you feel more discerning now?

Explore

- Practicing tuning in to spaces and things this week has taught me . . .

- Next time I feel an impulse to "get rid of," I will . . .

- I feel more discerning in these ways . . .

WEEK 12
CONNECTING WITH HOME

Love begins at home, and it is not how much we do ... but how much love we put into that action.
—Mother Teresa

DAY 78
WHAT HOME MEANS TO YOU

It doesn't take much for me to feel at home. Give me a comfy chair, surround me with beautiful objects, simmer me a pot of soup, soak me in a hot bath at the end of a long day, and I'm in heaven.

Home is not just a physical structure, but the sense that comes built into our human experience of feeling safe and whole. Home is what informs and gives meaning to our lives. Home and well-being go together.

As I see it, homes are not just these empty boxes that we fill with collections of stuff, life experiences, and unique personalities. They are alive and dynamic places that respond directly to our attentiveness (or lack thereof). Our homes and workplaces are extensions of us: they affect us, reflect us, support us. There is no separation.

What does home mean to you?

Explore
- To me, home means . . .
- I can improve my connection with my home by . . .

DAY 79
YOUR WEATHER MAP

Imagine that you are the weatherman on TV describing the weather patterns of your home. Would you describe it mostly enjoying fair and sunny skies, or cloudy weather and storms?

Do certain spaces feel cold, prickly, unsettled, chaotic, queasy, depressed, oppressed, noisy, constricted? Do others feel calm, warm, open, settled, coherent, quiet, alive, spacious? Do you notice yourself being drawn to some rooms or spaces more than others?

Yes, these patterns can all coexist under the same roof.

After you've had a chance to tune in to the weather map for your home, bring your attention to one or two rooms or spaces that feel "calmer" to you. What makes them feel calm in relation to others that don't feel so calm?

Use today to simply notice and not judge.

Explore
- The weather patterns of my home look and feel like . . . (and areas where I'm inclined to spend most of my time . . .)
- I notice these differences between spaces that calm me and those that do not . . .

DAY 80
TOUR OF THE HOME
MEDITATION—PART I

Today you will be taking a virtual guided tour of your home. This exercise is a favorite among my students because of how much it reveals. And the more you do it, the more you'll get out of it.

1. **Close your eyes.** Take an easy breath in, and a slow, empty-ing breath out. Breathe out all thought and tension. Breathe in pure awareness and possibility.

2. With each out breath, **expand** your personal energy field outward—that invisible part of you that radiates out from the physical body. Ask that your energy field be clear and unattached.

3. When you feel ready, **imagine** your expanded self standing at the front entrance of your home or apartment—whichever doorway you use the most. Before stepping over the thresh-old, take a moment to notice what it feels like here.

4. Now **take a step inside**. What is the first thing that catches your attention? Perhaps it is an object, or a smell, or the way the door opens . . .

5. Take a few minutes to **wander and explore**. Open doors and closets if you need to—just peek and poke around. Allow yourself to be guided and receive whatever informa-tion comes through your senses. *Note:* This meditation is purely a data-gathering mission. There is nothing you need to do other than notice the thoughts, feelings, and judg-ments that come up.

6. **Notice** smells, sounds, colors, temperature changes. Notice prickliness, smoothness, heaviness, lightness. Notice the spaces or objects that draw you in or repel you. Notice the things that you hadn't noticed before. Be aware of any dips in your energy level as you enter each space. Pay particular attention to any auditory, visual, or kinesthetic messages from your body, and trust your expanded self to recall these details when it's time to reflect on the experience in your journal.

7. When you feel complete, **return** to the doorway where you first entered.

8. **Bless your home** by surrounding her with love and golden light.

9. Step back out over the threshold, and **open your eyes**.

When you feel complete, take a few minutes to reflect on the experience in your journal using the prompts that follow.

Explore

- When I stood on the threshold of my home, I felt . . .
- Some of the spaces (objects) that drew me in right away were . . .
- Some of the spaces/objects that repelled me were . . .
- To bless my home, I . . .
- When I connect with her in this way, it feels . . .

DAY 81
TOUR OF THE HOME
MEDITATION—PART 2

Today you'll have an opportunity to fine-tune yesterday's data-gathering session of your home: You'll identify certain areas that could use some love and attention, learn what your home has to tell you, and outline specific steps you can take to support your home over the coming week.

1. **Repeat steps 1–6** of the Tour of the Home—Part 1.

2. **Be guided to one area** in your home or apartment that might register as contracted, stuck, tight, or tentative. You

might resonate with it or be repelled by it. Trust your fully expanded self to know exactly where to go.

3. **Take a seat** in an imaginary chair that has been placed for you in this space.

4. **Be aware** of your comfort level, knowing that you are completely safe right now. Notice your breathing and your heart rate.

5. **Listen closely**—this space wants to let you know what is working for her, and what isn't. Don't try to explain or defend; just listen unconditionally. Give this some time.

6. **Thank** the space for being honest. **Tell her** what you will do specifically to support her every day this week. Make your offer simple, doable, and heartfelt.

7. When you feel complete, get up from the chair and **return** to the doorway where you first entered; **bless** your home again, and **step back** over the threshold.

Were you surprised to land where you did? Give yourself a little extra time today to reflect on your second Tour of the Home using the prompts that follow.

Explore
- Walking through my home the second time felt like . . .
- The space where I landed was . . .
- She told me . . .
- What surprised me about this experience . . .
- I promised to support this space in the coming week in these ways . . .

DAY 82
HOMES AS MIRRORS

In yesterday's guided tour you had a chance to have a sit-down chat with a space in your home.

In what ways do you think this space was reflecting back an unloved or neglected aspect in *you?* How is your space mirroring an unfulfilled yearning?

Yes, the writing is on the walls. All you need to do is open your eyes.

Explore
- The areas in my life that have been neglected and unloved are reflected back to me by my home in these ways . . .
- My home is a reflection of me because . . .

DAY 83
WHEN ROCK BOTTOM HITS HOME (MINDING FEAR)

I've written scads on the subject of how our living spaces are affected by human emotions. Left unchecked, highly charged negative thoughts and feelings have a way of sticking around. Literally.

So what do you do when a loved one hits rock bottom in your home? What do you do when a torrent of unconscious and unprocessed pain has made its way into the walls and crevices of your home, head, and heart?

Let's look at an example from my friend, Albert:

We just spent a rather harrowing weekend at our house helping an old friend detox from acute alcoholism, and we feel that the house has some really bad energy stuck in it. All the ugliness of addiction, blame, loss, heartbreak, and bitterness seem to still be in our beautiful home. What can we do to encourage it to move on? We want to open all the windows and let all the air out.

Al was right to think that it isn't just us humans that are emotionally impacted by pain. Our homes get slammed, too. The impulse to open all the windows is a good one, but the most important thing to manage with clearing *anything* is fear. Being afraid of the disturbance, or acting out of worry, is like adding fuel to a fire.

It's not possible to banish "bad" energy. There's no big hole in the sky where it can go. When a space is disturbed, it means that the energies are noisy, chaotic, and out of balance. Fear cannot exist in the light of pure compassionate awareness.

Start with clearing the fears in you and the rest will follow. Revisiting the lessons in this book on the stories you tell yourself (Week 9) is a good place to shine light on your fears. The Simple Clearing Process from Day 61 will help to release them.

What fear are you still holding on to that could use some compassionate awareness today?

Explore
- A fear I am still holding on to is . . .
- This fear has made its way into my (our) home because . . .
- One thing I can do today to "love it up" is . . .

DAY 84
CHECK IN—CONNECTING WITH HOME

This week we connected with home in a deeper way by mapping its unique weather patterns, receiving its wisdom, and exploring what it reveals about us.

What does your home need more of? If you think of your home like the dear friend and loyal servant that it is, what is one thing you'd like to do to honor its unconditional service? It could be as simple as opening the windows and letting in some fresh air. Or it could be something more intentional, such as lighting a stick of incense, buying a bouquet of fresh flowers, or repeating your pledge of support.

Explore
- My home needs more of . . .
- My home serves me (us) by . . .
- One way I can honor my home's service on a regular basis is to . . .

WEEK 13
BEING ENOUGH

I'd been through so much, falling short again and again, and only recently had found a place where who I was, right now, was enough.
—Sarah Dessen, *The Truth About Forever*

DAY 85
STAY IN YOUR OWN LANE

We all do it.

In a dualistic world of better and worse, bigger and smaller, winners and losers, we all fall into an unconscious, unattractive habit of comparing ourselves to others.

I've put people on a pedestal because, well, they were obviously "more interesting" or "smarter" than me. They got to be on *Oprah,* had a gazillion likes on Facebook, had more manageable hair. I've gone the other way plenty too, placing myself high on that pedestal of gloating smugness. Ugh, just naming the truth of that feels awful.

Comparing is not just about putting people on a pedestal (or tearing them down) for their gifts and accomplishments. What interests me more is how we *dishonor ourselves* when we size up, measure, or take sides. When we make comparisons in this way, our true selves disappear. We separate and lose ourselves—especially when we're feeling vulnerable.

What are some of the ways you fall into the rabbit hole of feeling better than or lesser than? This quote by research professor and author Brené Brown might help you pull yourself back to center next time it happens: "Stay in your own lane. Comparison kills creativity and joy."

Explore
- I make myself better than or lesser than in these ways . . .
- Comparing myself to others makes me feel . . .

DAY 86
BREAK THE HABIT OF COMPARING

How do we know that we are enough just the way we are? How do we unplug from the comparing machine that takes us away from our truth and our center?

It's simple, really. Start by noticing when you compare, and then notice how you feel when you compare.

Whether you're feeling small (or puffed up), noticing your mouth going dry, or experiencing a shame wave (or a gloating one), the work is to stay with the sensations with as much compassionate awareness as you can until they pass.

Lots of practice clearing in this way can move mountains.

Explore
- My body's signals when I feel small or lesser than are . . .
- My body's signals when I'm feeling better than or puffed up are . . .

DAY 87
THERE'S NO COMPARISON MEDITATION

Today we're going to do a brief clearing practice that can help reduce the mind games of comparing.

1. **Close your eyes**, and take a nice, easy breath in, then a slow, emptying breath out.

2. When you feel centered, **recall a time** when you compared yourself to someone else. Perhaps it was a coworker, a sibling, or that "perfect" somebody who appears to have it all (or who you feel is beneath you).

3. **Ask yourself** what this person has, does, or says that makes you feel small and less than (or better than).

4. **Observe** where in your body you feel contracted, and allow any and all sensations of smallness (or grandeur) to arise without taking them personally. Notice your breathing.

5. When you feel complete, **tune in to** a positive quality about this person. For example, it could be how he or she lights up a room, gives generously, or makes people laugh.

6. Take another deep breath and **reflect on** how this person reminds you of you; how this person mirrors back an aspect, value, or deeper yearning that *already exists in you* (that you've been tamping down).

7. When you feel complete, **open your eyes** and notice how you're feeling. Notice your breathing. Notice if you're feeling differently from when you started.

Deepen your experience of the meditation by reflecting on the prompts that follow in your journal. And remember, the trick is to repeat the process until you've rewired the pattern. You'll know it's gone when the situation or person no longer elicits a charge.

Explore

- A person who has made me feel "less than" or "better than" is . . .

- Comparing myself to him/her feels . . .

- A positive quality about this person is . . .
- This person reminds me of me in these ways . . .

DAY 88
YOU ARE ENOUGH

Get this: You are perfect just as you are. There is nothing you need to do, or fix, or change about yourself.

This doesn't mean that you won't be growing and evolving. What it means is simply that you are whole and complete just as you are. Now.

Take it in. It's yours.

Explore
- In this moment there is nothing I need to do, fix, or change about myself because . . . (Embrace the squeamish part of you that doesn't quite own it yet.)
- One thing that can help me remember that I am whole and complete just as I am . . .

DAY 89
REFLECTIONS ON BEING ENOUGH

What makes clearing so powerful is when people share their heart-felt experiences of the journey. Case in point, this eloquent posting from Laura T. describes making peace with what it means to be "good enough." Personal stories like these help us all come out of hiding and lighten our collective loads:

What's beginning to "bubble up" is that clutter is ANYthing that holds me back from my best self and best life (for me, my own idiosyncratic definition of "best"). In fact, oftentimes my definition of "best" is "good enough," and that works well.

But not always. My body wasn't in complete broken-down mode, so it was, although fat, "good enough" to get me around. But was it my "best" body that I could achieve realistically? No, not even close. And even if I wanted to put my metaphoric hands over my ears and sing *la la la la la,* I also knew that my middle-aged body was teetering on the brink of diabetes (thankfully not there yet), a knee replacement, and other fun stuff.

So clearing my mental clutter is shifting this mindset from just good enough to better than that to some form of best for me.

So how do we embrace the concept of enough—as in being enough, having enough, and knowing that there is enough to go around? These simple phrases might help: "I am enough. I have enough. There is enough."

Next time you find yourself getting snagged by comparison, desire, and/or attachment, close your eyes and repeat one or all three of these phrases out loud. Allow them to soften belief patterns of scarcity that cloud the truth of who you are.

How do you feel now knowing that enough is enough?

Explore
- I know that I am enough because . . .
- I know that I have enough because . . .
- I know there is always enough to go around because . . .

DAY 90
MIRROR NOT REQUIRED

There's a quote that's been floating around the Internet for quite some time that says, "Many people would be scared if they saw in the mirror not their faces, but their character." This got me thinking, What if people could also see the clutter that they carry in their personal energy field? That would be quite a mirror.

Truth is, there is no hiding stress. Or stuckness. Or fear.

It is visible.

There is no mirror needed to reflect back our innate clarity, either.

The shimmering, sparkly light that we are is unmistakable.

Explore
- My stuck self looks and feels like . . .
- My shimmering, sparkly light looks and feels like . . .

DAY 91
CHECK IN—BEING ENOUGH

This week you had an opportunity to shift the paradigm around being and having enough and rewire the part of the brain that is still attached to comparing and scarcity.

What helps you remember to stay in your own lane and stop comparing yourself to others? What is something you can do today to celebrate the perfection that is your being, and the infinite abundance that is your life?

Explore

- What helps me remember to stay in my own lane . . .
- One thing I can do today to celebrate and honor myself is . . .

WEEK 14
MOVING THINGS, MOVING ON

I want to shed my waste with quiet reverence like the pine ...

Keep me mindful of what I take into my home, the items bought to substitute for real living ... Help me slowly to surrender all excess.
—Gunilla Norris, *Being Home*

DAY 92
PRESS THE REFRESH BUTTON

No sooner had my husband and I returned from a six-month sabbatical in Mexico than we went on a top-to-bottom tear of reorganizing our entire home. We had barely unpacked our bags.

What prompted the sudden and unexpected musical-chairs makeover became very clear: Spending time away from home has a way of changing your perspective. Big time. Things just didn't feel right. Energetically we had expanded, while the house and its contents had not budged an inch.

Many of our clothes looked tired. Art and furniture felt stagnant in places. My north-facing home office was too cave-like to inspire any writing about lightening up. Our TV had not caught up with the twenty-first century.

It wasn't just things that needed changing up. Moving things also meant moving on, which in our case meant embracing a new chapter as empty nesters. There is no getting around the past when everything in the home points to it.

What is one thing you can move for one minute today? Use this simple task of moving one thing to anchor the sense that you can *move on* from whatever it is that's holding you back.

Yes, moving things to move things forward can be as simple as that.

Explore
- I'm ready to move on without these things in my life . . .
- One thing I can move today to get things going is . . .

DAY 93
MAKEOVER REVEALS

When my husband and I decided to move our entire house around, we had no big game plan. It evolved organically.

Clothing and household items went first. Sentimental attachments, like the shoes I wore only once at my wedding, made their way into piles without a second thought.

We rehung artwork that elevated us, replaced pieces that we no longer loved.

We upgraded our TV with a super sleek model that does just about everything but cook your meals. In the spirit of "one thing in, one thing out," I cleaned up the small TV, put it out on the curb, and sold it for forty bucks the same day.

We were on a roll. Moving things out of the house gave us the umph to keep moving forward onto bigger ideas that proved to be even more radical, like repurposing some of our rooms. We moved my entire home office—desks, file cabinets, shelves, books—into our daughter's childhood bedroom and put her things into my former workspace. Turns out the north-facing orientation makes it perfect for sleeping. Who knew?

You never know what might be revealed when you move things around. It might lead to a nurturing nook of a space you didn't realize you needed (and always wanted), or fresh uses for things that you already own (and never used).

You may just feel like you've moved into a new home without ever actually having to.

Explore

- Something I can move around today to see what might be revealed is . . .
- One thing I didn't know I needed until I began this journey is . . .

DAY 94
BRING FRESH EYES

There are a couple ways to bring fresh eyes to an old situation before you begin moving things around.

First, you can repeat the Tour of the Home meditations (see Days 80 and 81) with the specific intention of seeing something in your home or life with fresh eyes.

Second, you can go away for a few days with the intention of having fresh eyes when you return.

Either way, ask yourself:

- What doesn't feel right? What seems off?
- What can I change about my space right now?
- What am I ready to let go of today?
- Who can help me?

Allow the answers to these questions to reveal themselves as you move about your home. Don't think too much. Use your six senses to inform and illuminate.

Once you've identified an area that needs attention (and lined up some support if necessary), ask to be shown the first step you can take to address the situation. What does your first step look like?

Explore

- When I bring fresh eyes to an area of my home, I notice . . .
- My first step in making a change is looking like . . .

DAY 95
YOU DON'T HAVE TO BE A MINIMALIST

Here is a short list of basic truths about having and managing our possessions (in no particular order):

- Things look a lot worse when they're spread out all over the place and haven't yet been put away.
- You don't have to be a minimalist for your space to feel clear.
- A space feels good when your things make your heart sing, add value, and are placed with intention.
- Things without a home are clutter.

If you're wondering why I'd bother stating the obvious, here's why: To a clear and rational mind, things make perfect sense. But to a stressed-out mind, I might as well be speaking in tongues. Taking a step back and looking at your living situation and your life dispassionately can lead to fresh insights.

Explore

- The truth that speaks to me the most is . . . (because . . .)
- The truth that challenges me the most is . . . (because . . .)

DAY 96
SIXTY-SECOND ROUND UP

If you want a clearing exercise that delivers a big bang for your buck, I invite you to try one of my favorites. It's called the Sixty-Second Round Up:

1. **Round up one thing, pile, or area** for one minute every day for a week.
2. **Pick a spot:** Choose an area that looks like a tornado hit it (or isn't quite up to your desired standards): your desktop, kids' toys, the fridge, your car . . .
3. For best effect, **choose the same** area and time every day.
4. **Set a timer** if you need one, and notice the energy in the space (and in you) before, during, and after your clearing.
5. **Have fun!**

This simple daily practice helps to calm the fight-or-flight response and builds new neural pathways in the brain that make clearing increasingly doable and effortless.

Tailor this exercise to suit your needs. For example, if it feels like too much to round up a whole room or area, **reduce** the round-up perimeter to smaller areas or piles in your home. Conversely, if it's too easy to do one room, **expand** the round-up to include other piles or spaces in your home.

Explore
- One area I can easily round up for sixty seconds every day this week is . . .
- The idea of repeating the same task for a week feels . . .

DAY 97
EASY DOES IT

You don't need to go full-throttle, go away for six months, or have a life partner to refresh your home. If you're willing to take it on as a journey that you experience instead of a task that you have to complete by a certain deadline, you'll get on a roll too.

The key is to keep tasks small and simple. Follow the rule of one: address one thing, one pile, or one area in your home for one minute every day—with awareness.

Pay particular attention to your breathing, and how the energy feels before, during, and after. Repeat this every day until the process becomes natural and effortless.

Explore
- When I reduce a task to one minute and repeat it, I notice . . .
- When I insert awareness into a task and repeat it, I feel . . .

DAY 98
CHECK IN—MOVING THINGS, MOVING ON

The focus this week was to see how moving things around creates greater ease, flow, and openings that we never could have imagined before. Simple repetitive practices help us gather the loose ends of our home and our life.

How has adopting a simple daily practice of moving things around helped you become more balanced and aware? Have you noticed an increase (or decrease) in motivation to clear other areas of your home and life? In what ways do you feel less scattered (or more) this week?

Explore

- Moving things around every day this week has helped me . . .
- I feel more (or less) motivated this week . . . (because . . .)
- Ways that I feel less (or more) scattered this week . . .

WEEK 15
INVITING CALM

Breathing in, I calm my body. Breathing out, I smile.
—Thich Nhat Hanh, *Present Moment Wonderful Moment*

DAY 99
RINGING PHONES

Ringing phones jangle me. If you saw the way I flinch and lose focus, you'd think it was the president himself calling from the Oval Office to say the country was in a state of emergency. And I *must* respond. Or at least check to see who's calling so "urgently."

It doesn't matter if it's my phone or someone else's, if it has a beautiful ringtone or is set on vibrate; the effect on my nervous system is exactly the same.

What happens to your breathing (and your state of mind) when any of your devices ring, ping, or vibrate?

Next time your phone rings, use it as an opportunity to take a deep breath . . . in . . . and . . . out . . . for five seconds before you check to see who's calling. Notice and breathe into the discomfort of needing to know.

Explore
- When my devices ring, my breathing becomes . . .
- Postponing my need to know feels . . .

DAY 100
WELCOME CALM

Our devices give us a terrific opportunity to practice cultivating calm. Here's how one of my students, Withpaint (an alias), has made friends with her phone and computer:

> I have changed how I use my phone now. When I am taking time to be with someone, I put my phone on quiet and out of sight. I limit my time on the computer, and have a sign on it that asks, "What else could you be doing now?" . . . I took FB [the Facebook app] off my phone. It can wait until I have that spare time to catch up with what is happening. I do not need to know every day, every minute what is happening to my friends, and although I love learning about herbs/feminist issues/news/cute animal tricks . . . they now have a place and time.

What is one way that you find calm in your life?

Use today to practice cultivating calm. Call it in. Step into it. Invite it in, like an old friend you haven't seen in a while.

Explore
- One thing that calms me is . . .
- Calling calm into my life feels . . .

DAY 101
PHONE HOME

In his beautiful book of mindfulness verses, *Present Moment Wonderful Moment*, Buddhist teacher Thich Nhat Hanh offers an alternative way to answer the phone:

When the telephone rings, the bell creates in us a kind of vibration, maybe some anxiety: "Who is calling? Is it good news or bad news?" . . .

The next time you hear the phone ring, I recommend that you stay exactly where you are, and become aware of your breathing: "Breathing in, I calm my body. Breathing out, I smile."

How does it feel just to say those words out loud?

Explore
- To breathe in calm and breathe out peace feels . . .
- When I use Thich Nhat Hanh's phrase before answering the phone, I feel . . .

DAY 102
SHALLOW BREATHING

Maybe it's not a ringing phone that sends you into fight-or-flight. Maybe it's walking into a room that is a cluttered nightmare of piles everywhere. Maybe it's being late for an appointment, or having to confront a difficult family member or coworker.

Use today to connect the dots: Identify and write down the situations that cause your breathing to contract and grow shallow. This can be very subtle.

See what happens to your breathing when you witness it without attachment.

Explore
- These days, situations like these send me into fight-or-flight . . .
- My breathing becomes shallow when . . .

- When I witness my breathing without attachment, this happens . . .

DAY 103
CALMING MEDITATION

Today, practice this one-minute meditation. It is a simple and powerful exercise to quiet the mind and deepen the breath.

1. **Close your eyes**, and take a nice, easy breath in and a slow, emptying breath out . . . Breathe out all thought and tension. Breathe in pure awareness and possibility.
2. **Notice and allow** how you are feeling at this moment, without judging it as good or bad, or taking it personally.
3. **Repeat** Thich Nhat Hanh's phrases slowly, matching the pace of your breathing: "Breathing in, I calm my body. Breathing out, I smile."
4. After a minute has passed, or when you feel complete, **open your eyes.**
5. **Notice** how your body feels. Notice what goes through your mind.

Can you hear me now? ;-)

Explore
- Before the meditation, I was feeling . . .
- When I repeat Thich Nhat Hanh's breathing mantra, I feel . . .
- I feel most calm when . . .

DAY 104
FULLY FUNDED

As two self-employed worker bees who never know where the next check is coming from, my husband and I have an affirmation that we use to support our feeling spacious and calm around money. It was inspired by our good friend Desda Zuckerman, and it has never failed us:

My life is fully funded by the Bank of God.

Try it: Close your eyes and repeat this phrase out loud. What does it feel like to know that some greater force out there has your back, that your life is unconditionally covered?

Here's the thing about money: We cannot manifest a good livelihood without being willing to receive it.

Explore
- Saying "I am fully funded by the Bank of God" out loud feels . . .
- I trust that a greater force out there has my back because . . . (Acknowledge the part of you that is not so sure.)

DAY 105
CHECK IN—INVITING CALM

The focus this week was to invite calm and receptivity by using simple tools, like our phones, to practice breathing and mindfulness. No one sums the heart of the practice more beautifully than my online student, Veronika B., with this inspiration here (she credits Jayem's *Way of Mastery*): "Breathing in calm I have learned and used the following mantra for years now, though I still forget: Breath first, mind last, heart and feeling in the middle."

In what ways do you feel calmer this week? What are you ready to receive more of in your life?

Explore
- I feel more (or less) calm this week in these ways . . .
- I am ready to receive more of this in my life . . .

WEEK 16
TURNING UP THE LIGHT

Light reveals us to ourselves.
—Anne Lamott, *Help, Thanks, Wow*

DAY 106
MOOD ELEVATORS

Generally speaking, the journey of clearing is about releasing things, not acquiring them; letting go, not holding on. That said, it is also true that material objects that make your heart sing are not clutter. If they brighten your day, help you feel supremely good, connect you to a quiet place within, they are not clutter—or an extravagance.

As I reflect on the things that lift and nourish me, I could probably come up with a whole slew that make my day every day. One of my favorites is twinkly lights. They are a mood elevator on a string, and one of the best inventions ever! I have a 100-bulb strand draped in my kitchen and one framing my back porch. As soon as it starts getting dark, *bling!*, on they go, making every day a holiday in my house.

What lifts your spirits? What helps you feel lighter and in the flow? What turns up the light in your life and helps you feel more spacious?

Explore
- One thing that lifts my spirits and lightens my load is . . .
- This thing makes me feel . . .

DAY 107
LIKE ATTRACTS LIKE

What are you vibrating?

If you are vibrating at the level of "poor me," "there's not enough to go around," "I'm afraid for my kids, my future, my life"—or any thought or fear—guess what you're going to get more of?

Conversely, guess what you'll get if you're vibrating at the level of "I trust the universe to supply me with what I need when I need it."

You do the math. It's your choice. As always.

Explore

- Right now I'm vibrating at the level of . . .
- One thing I can do today to raise it up a notch . . .

DAY 108
IT'S ALL RIGHT

What goes through your head when you read the following words by Abraham-Hicks?

> If you knew everything was really all right, and that it always has a happy ending, then you would not feel trepidacious [sic] about your future. Everything is really so very all right! If you could believe and trust that, then, immediately everything would automatically and instantly become all right.

Did you feel a gulp or get snagged by the concept of everything having a happy ending? Feel the charge, feel the resistance, and let it go. That is the work.

Explore
- When I see the words "happy ending," I feel . . .
- I know that everything is really all right because . . . (Notice the part that isn't so sure.)

DAY 109
CONFIDENCE BOOSTERS

What helps you feel confident? What boosts you when you start to contract, collapse, or cave in?

I posed these questions to the brilliant circle of students on my *DailyOM* course, "A Year to Clear What's Holding You Back!" and this is what some of them had to say:

I feel it when I finish a project. I lose it when procrastination takes over and I make excuses for not making progress. Through this course and all the other inspirational messages out there, I am seeing my light shine within. And with all the light within us, we are beacons in this world. So shine on. (Julie T.)

Surrender was my way last night. I could see how much I still strive, effort, and try hard, etc. Yet I long to go with the flow. I can't swim upstream and downstream at the same time. As I surrendered, ease came to me, and with it, trust. And trust IS confidence. (Veronika B., inspired by Abraham-Hicks)

What boosts me when I contract—if I am aware enough to notice that contraction and I challenge its truth or lack of it as the feeling unfolds—[is that] I can often talk myself out of the spiral of eroding confidence. As we have shared here, a lot of this insecurity is just . . . not . . . true! Come to think of it, sharing those collapsing feelings in a supportive environment helps a lot too. (Linda Z.)

On those days when you're feeling a little wobbly in the confidence department, or your self-esteem takes a hit, you can go deeper by asking yourself this question: What am I ready to cast aside today that might allow (even a peephole of) my dazzling light to come through?

Explore
- What helps me feel confident and light . . .
- I'm ready to cast aside . . .

DAY 110
YOUR BEST SELF

What words would you describe your best self? Write them down on a piece of paper or in your journal. Choose one of the words and focus your attention on it today. Without apology.

Explore
- Words that describe my best self . . .
- Naming them without apology feels . . .

DAY 111
WHAT WOULD YOU DO?

What if I told you that you are one hundred percent worthy?

Yes, worthy. As in deserving of love, kindness, abundance, respect, joy.

One size fits all.

Explore

- What I would do if I knew that I was 100 percent worthy . . .
- What would change if I knew that I was 100 percent worthy . . .

DAY 112
CHECK IN—TURNING UP THE LIGHT

The focus this week was to "turn up the light" in our homes and lives by remembering these simple truths: All is well, there are no mistakes, and we attract at the level that we vibrate.

Raising our personal vibration is a choice that is easier to make the more we cultivate well-being and worthiness.

In what ways do you recognize the light that you are? What does it feel like to shine your light more brightly, without apology? In what ways do you know for sure that all is well?

Explore

- I recognize my light in these ways . . .
- To shine more brightly feels . . .
- I know that I have nothing to worry about because . . .

ℜ

WEEK 17
SOUL CALLING

When you want something, all the universe conspires in helping you to achieve it.
—Paulo Coelho, *The Alchemist*

DAY 113
GIVING UP DOESN'T PAY

In 2007, I published my first book. It was a thing of beauty. What most people don't know is that bringing my baby into the world took about ten years. And then some. The arc of the journey looked something like this:

I wrote: A lot.

I prepared: I took classes on how to write a book proposal and stellar query letter.

I pitched: I sent my stellar query letter to two dozen literary agents.

I crumpled: I was (graciously) rejected by every single one.

I revived: I found the strength to pick myself up, gather what I'd learned, and press on.

I recommitted: I took the entire book apart, opened up a new Word document, and started again.

I celebrated: I self-published. Sold many copies. Got the attention of a publisher. Received a book contract to create a new and improved edition.

I began again.

Those are just the highlights, of course. The *real* story that this abbreviated chronology is not telling could be more simply summarized with these **simple truths about a soul journey**:

1. Journeys do not always add up, make sense, or go in a straight line.
2. Every obstacle informs, and every step matters.
3. When you feel lost, you aren't. You just can't see what's up ahead.

It would take me years to see the unfolding of a bigger picture, and hindsight to appreciate the potential impact of bailing on my dream.

If I had quit, there would be no book on which to build a platform. Without the experience of a no, I would never experience the sweetness of a yes—a yes that would eventually lead to teaching and reaching a whole lot more people with books like this one.

So you see, it doesn't pay to give up on your dreams.

The dream machine is leaving the station. The time is now. What are you ready to take a chance on? What is holding you back?

Explore
- I'm ready to take a chance on . . .
- I believe this is what's holding me back from acting . . .
- Taking a chance has paid off in the past when I've . . .

DAY 114
GATHERING BEAUTY

There's a potent energy when we gather the things we love in one place—even if they're just pictures of the real thing.

One of my favorite places to organize what I love through pictures is Pinterest. It's a personalized online gallery that you decorate and populate with things, places, and ideas that interest you.

From jaw-dropping photographs to laugh-out-loud cartoons, I now have over thirty collections ranging from cozy and sparkling home spaces to simple organizing solutions, dreamy landscapes, guilty pleasures, inspiring books, and amazing art. Beautiful photographs do wonders for my soul. I am soothed and expanded when I steep in their beauty and move them around.

What soothes and expands you? What makes your heart sing?

Explore
- These are some things that soothe and expand me . . .
- These things make my heart sing . . .

DAY 115
PICTURE THE LIFE YOU WANT

Making ideal image posters, or vision boards, from photos, images, or words is a powerful way to play with intention. It can help to visualize, get clear, act "as if," organize our life, see everything in one place, make room for ourselves. When a vision board is a vibrational match, it can help us remember what we love, what we want to attract, and where we want to be going.

It's not difficult to picture the life you want. Start by gathering images that make your heart sing and place them on a poster board, bulletin board, or refrigerator door. Look at them every day for at least a minute. Imbibe their energizing power and beauty.

Watch what happens when you allow the reflections of your best self to shine through and work their magic.

Explore

- When I picture the life I want, I see . . .
- Words and images that support this desire are . . .

DAY 116
HOW TO REALIZE YOUR DREAM

Today's a big day. Are you ready? Because I'm going to offer you my best tips for realizing your dream (or anything, for that matter)—whether it is writing your memoir, shedding those twenty pounds, or living in a clutter-free home:

1. **Be clear** on what you really want: Write it down and define what it looks like. Feel your desire down to your bones. Once fired up, the intention machine will deliver the goods. Be sure you want them.

2. **Act as if** your dream home (job, relationship, body) already exists. Enliven it with all of your senses. If it's publishing a book, for example, *see* yourself at a book signing; *feel* the soreness in your hands from signing hundreds of books; *hear* your fans gushing over your gleaming book cover and beautiful headshot.

3. **Do one thing a day** (preferably at the same time every day) that moves you closer to your dream. Adopt the phrase "I choose ease" as your mantra.

4. **Keep your tasks simple** so as not to elicit a stress response. If you notice yourself feeling overwhelmed or losing hope, dial it back. Think "doable" just for today, and allow the next step to reveal itself.

5. **Stay true to your self** and try not to let other people's opinions, and your own critical mind, sway you. The part of the

mind that doesn't like change has a way of derailing our best efforts by drawing to us people and situations that don't serve or support us. Try not to give in to the noise.

6. **Be aware of transitions**. Sometimes as we get close to realizing our dreams, we might bump up against some resisting behaviors. If you feel more cranky than usual, or are ready to throw in the towel, this could be a sign that you are about ready to birth something big. Hang in there!

7. **Let go of attachment to the outcome.** Attachment stops the flow of energy. Letting it go creates openings and opportunities that could lead you places beyond your wildest imaginings.

8. **Be open and have fun!** Allow the magic of your deepest intentions to reveal itself.

Close your eyes for a moment and ask your soul what it wants to do today. Take a minute or two to listen, and then follow through using these eight tips as your guide.

Explore
- Today my soul is calling forth . . .
- One thing I can do now to move toward realizing my dream is . . .

DAY 117
THROW YOUR DREAMS INTO SPACE

In her diary, Anaïs Nin writes,

> Throw your dream into space like a kite, and you do not know what it will bring back, a new life, a new friend, a new love, a new country.

Spend a minute today casting your deepest hopes and dreams into the wind, like seeds. Let them go with fluidity and ease. Ask to be shown signs of new growth and life in ways that you will easily recognize.

Explore
- Today I'm casting these seeds . . .
- I'm seeing these signs of growth . . .

DAY 118
CAN YOU RECEIVE?

Of the many pearls of wisdom that have been uttered by the wise and generous Oprah Winfrey, it is this question that works on me every time I land on it: "Can you allow yourself to receive the fullness of your success?"

Can you allow yourself to receive what you most desire? Can you allow yourself to receive divine inspiration? Can you allow yourself to receive the universe's abundance of riches and blessings?

For me, the answer, of course, would be yes! *That* would be success. So why is it so hard to receive? Why do we choose scarcity over fullness? Why do we play it safe and act smaller than we truly are? Maybe those are the questions we should be asking (and clearing).

Explore
- It is safe for me to allow myself to receive because . . .
- Breathing in fullness feels like . . .
- I am infinitely deserving of everything I most desire because . . . (Notice the part of you that doesn't quite believe it yet.)

DAY 119
CHECK IN—SOUL CALLING

If we were to peel away all the layers of our physical, mental, and emotional self, what we would be left with is the core of our being—that immutable, divinely guided, infinitely intelligent essence that makes us the unique beings that we are: our soul.

This week was an opportunity connect with the soul: to clarify and anchor our deepest dreams in ways that the heart can relate to; receive fully what we most desire; and make room for our soul's true calling by letting go of attachment to specific outcomes.

What have you learned this week about your soul? How do you know when your soul is calling?

Explore

- It is my soul's yearning to . . .
- I know when my soul is calling because . . .
- Times that I have followed through on my soul's calling . . . (and how it made me feel . . .)

WEEK 18
LETTING GO, LETTING FLOW

The starting point is realizing that letting go is not a dramatic
moment we build up to some time in the future. It is happening
now, in the present moment—it is not singular but ongoing.
—Judy Lief, "How to Let Go"

DAY 120
FAVORITE SONG

There's an adorable sepia photograph that made the rounds on Facebook
a while back of a little girl standing in front of a street musician. With
arms flung up and bent backward, she appears to be in total ecstasy. The
caption reads: "How I feel when my favorite song comes on."

That's me in a nutshell. If a song comes on the radio that I adore,
chances are I'm going to swoon, if not rise out of my chair in unmitigated joy like I'm at a revival meeting.

What makes you lose yourself in joy, even for just a few seconds?

Try it: Dance or move to one of your favorite songs today with the
intention of releasing a thing, a thought, or an issue that makes you feel
stuck.

Be loose. Be liquid. Be yourself.

Explore
- Songs that make me swoon . . .
- What makes me lose myself in joy . . .

DAY 121
WHAT DOES SPACIOUSNESS FEEL LIKE?

If I were to describe what spaciousness feels like to me, it would be something like this:

- Frictionless: like sitting in a glider rocking chair.
- Buoyant: floating in the warm sea.
- Perfectly synced: when all the green lights sync up perfectly, or when things work out perfectly without my having to try so hard.
- Cozy: crawling into a warm bed after taking a hot bath.
- In awe: the rush I get when a huge plane takes off.
- In joy: laughing so hard it hurts.
- Effortless ease: when nothing sticks, jangles, rankles, hurts, or perturbs.
- Trusting: feeling held by the divine order of things.

Spaciousness isn't just a concept. It is a tangible and sensory state of being that you can tap into and cultivate.

What does spaciousness feel like to you?

Explore
- What spaciousness feels like to me . . .
- Times in my life when I have felt most spacious . . .

DAY 122
MELT INTO SPACIOUSNESS

As I see it, melting is what being human is all about: Melting attachments. Melting unfinished business. Melting fear. Melting resistance. Melting into Oneness. Melting into the truth of who we really are . . .

Melting.

Yes. It can be that easy. When we allow it.

What is your soul wanting to melt into today? Allow it.

Explore

- My soul wants to melt into this today . . .
- What it feels like when I allow it . . .

DAY 123
HOW FLUID CAN YOU BE?

I am mesmerized by this black-and-white video on YouTube of a guy dancing in a backlit space to Parov Stelar's song, "All Night." There is something about the way he moves with effortless ease that puts me in a delicious trance. He's liquid motion. Or butter.

Try it: Spend a minute today watching the steam undulating from your tea—or a cat, a baby, anything or anyone that moves with complete fluidity and ease.

Watch and learn. These are great teachers.

Explore

- Watching fluidity makes me feel . . .
- When I'm fluid, I feel . . .

DAY 124
SPACIOUS MAGIC

I feel it when I put the dishes away, fold the laundry, or fluff up the sofa and pillows before going to bed at night. It is the spacious infusion that results from housekeeping rituals that I repeat every day.

Realized and harnessed by simply being aware.

When you insert awareness into any ordinary task, and repeat it every day, you create a sense of ease and fluidity that can only be described as effortless, spacious magic.

Try it: Choose a daily housekeeping task that you usually do on autopilot. Insert pure awareness for at least one minute. Repeat this every day for a week, and see if this simple daily tending doesn't lead to an opening—a peephole of spacious ease—that wasn't there before.

Explore
- A daily task that I can take on as an experiment to cultivate spacious magic is . . .
- When I insert pure awareness into the task, I notice . . .

DAY 125
TRY SOMETHING DIFFERENT

It doesn't take much to move stuck energy. Sometimes just making a slight pivot in a new direction for a few days can help break up some old, stuck patterns.

You could take a different route to work, or go left instead of taking your usual right turn in the supermarket aisle, for example. You could get up fifteen minutes earlier, or lollygag in bed fifteen minutes longer. You could shower in the evening instead of the morning, or sleep on the left side of the bed instead of the right. You could have a cup of tea with honey instead of your usual coffee, cream, and two sugars.

You could respond instead of react.

As the Sufi poet Rumi reminds us, "Very little grows on jagged rock." What is something different you can try today that will help you loosen up some of the crusty stuff?

Explore

- Something new I can try today is . . .
- Going off-road a little bit from my usual routine feels . . .

DAY 126
CHECK IN—LETTING GO, LETTING FLOW

The focus this week was to loosen and melt some of the crusty resistances that keep you stuck in old ways. The poetry of the thirteenth-century Sufi mystic Rumi is particularly helpful with this. Trying something new that doesn't activate the fight-or-flight response can also break up stuck patterns.

What has helped you feel greater fluidity, ease, and spacious detachment this week?

Explore

- Being more fluid feels . . .
- Some simple housekeeping tasks I can do to help me cultivate spaciousness are . . .

WEEK 19
FILTERS AND PERCEPTIONS

We do not see things as they are, we see them as we are.
—Anaïs Nin, *Seduction of the Minotaur*

DAY 127
MISSED PERCEPTION

A number of years ago, the *Washington Post* conducted a social experiment. They had Joshua Bell, a world-class violinist, play six Bach pieces in a DC Metro station during rush hour. In forty-five minutes, thousands of people walked past him, and only six stopped to listen. About twenty gave him money. When he finished, no one noticed, and no one applauded.

On his blog, Jeff Bridges (yes, *that* Jeff Bridges—The Dude) framed this experiment by asking what this tells us about perception:

In a common place environment at an inappropriate hour, do we perceive beauty?

Do we stop to appreciate it?

Do we recognize talent in an unexpected context?

I want to think I would have stopped and appreciated Joshua Bell's artistry and skill, but I probably would have walked right by, too busy worrying about getting to an appointment or catching the next train.

Imagine what we might see and experience if we simply slowed down a little bit. If seeing more "out there" is a function of how clear we are within, imagine the beauty that would *not* go unnoticed.

Now that's an experiment worth trying.

Explore
- Beauty I'm noticing right now . . .
- One way I can invite more beauty into my life is . . .

DAY 128
POLARIZING FILTERS

You don't need to know much about photography to know that the viewfinder of a camera will capture what it sees, and the shutter will click on a moment, freezing it in linear space and time. The more sophisticated photographer can manipulate and control the outcome of her images by increasing or decreasing the shutter speed, by adjusting the aperture, and by adding different lenses and filters. By mounting a polarizing filter, for instance, she can remove the harsh glare to create a richer, darker, more textured shot. A telephoto or macro lens can capture sharp detail; a fisheye lens creates an interesting, distorted fishbowl.

What do your inner lenses and filters look like? To what extent have you amplified, enhanced, distorted, blurred, cropped, or polarized the reality of who you are? What does your world look like through your "rose-cluttered" glasses?

Better yet, what does your world look like when they're clear?

Explore
- One thing I can see with greater clarity about myself since I began this book is . . .
- One way my clearing is changing the way I see myself and the world is . . .

DAY 129
POPPING PERCEPTIONS

In response to the question, "What is bubbling up since you began your clearing journey?" a student responded with a very creative suggestion—one which seemed, coincidently, to bubble up on the spot (thank you for this wisdom, Tammy!):

As I asked myself the question, "What has been bubbling up?" my initial response was, "Nothing, yet" . . .

Then, within the disappointment in myself for not integrating anything mentally or having the time to physically DO something to support the lessons while they were fresh in my head, the image of a bubble stayed with me.

Could I possibly release thoughts or ideas into my own beautiful bubbles, and then, one by one, release each bubble into the air? We all know that bubbles do pop in reality, and I will allow my personal ones to pop, too.

That pop would then release my idea/thought, again. I will watch where it goes in its newfound freedom. If it comes close to me as it falls, I can choose to consciously catch it and reclaim it, or just let it go, allowing it to fall away from me. Its energy will return to the earth, where it is neither good nor bad . . . . It will just be neutral energy since it is no longer powered by me and my own perceptions and beliefs.

Hmmmmm . . . I think I will try this :-)

Don't you just love how the creative mind supplies us with what we need?

What "perception bubble" would you like to pop today?

Explore

- A perception that doesn't serve me that I could release today is . . .
- When I contain the thought in a bubble and watch it float away (and pop), I can feel myself . . .

DAY 130
CLUTTER CLOUD

In my first book *Your Spacious Self*, I adopted the adorable *Peanuts* cartoon character Pig-Pen (with his permanent cloud of dust) to describe the subtle energy field of a cluttered human:

> To the degree that we are carting around a lifetime of limiting beliefs, emotional attachments, and all those aspects in ourselves that we suppress, resist, and deny—also known as "shadow"—we're not all that different from that cute little guy. The bigger our shadow, the smoggier, denser, and, dare I say, not-so-cute this invisible "cloud."

These smoggy layers affect our thoughts, actions, and relationships. They become the filter through which we see and make choices.

What have you been carting around that you're ready to release right now?

Explore

- One thing in my life that has overstayed its welcome is . . .
- When I think about letting it go, I feel . . .

DAY 131
STRINGS ATTACHED

By now you probably know that I'm a big fan of metaphors to illustrate what is going on energetically when our homes and lives are out of balance. You can blame it on twenty years as a high school teacher.

Here's another one for your consideration: Imagine one object that you don't use or love equals one invisible string. A negative thought equals another string. Over time, these unnecessary objects, negative thoughts, addictions, unmitigated fears, and painful memories, cycled over and over again, equal a stringy mess.

A stringy mess that we spin out of our energy field like a spider's web.

If this concept is agitating you right now (as it is me), take it as a sign to stop, name, and feel. And breathe.

Let it all go. These strings are not who you are.

Explore
- Right now I'm feeling . . .
- One thing I can do to ease the pressure is . . .

DAY 132
STATIC CLING

The thing about having a personal energy field that is smoggy like Pig-Pen's is that it doesn't just travel with us everywhere we go. This invisible clutter cloud has two other distinguishing features as well:

- It has a powerful magnetic field that attracts more low-frequency energies like itself to itself.
- It leaves behind an energetic trail for others to attract and stick to.

The good news is that by clearing one thing or thought every day with compassionate awareness, you effectively discharge the stressful buildup in yourself, in others, and in the world at large.

Explore

- I know that clearing something affects others and changes the energy in my space because . . .
- How I know this to be true is . . .

DAY 133
CHECK IN—FILTERS AND PERCEPTIONS

The focus this week was to explore the concept of obscuration: how our beliefs and actions cloud and filter the truth of who we are. Thinking of clutter as Pig-Pen's dust swarm or as threads of a spider's web helps us understand its more pervasive, invisible impact.

The sensing practices in this book are designed to give you new and sustainable ways to know (feel) how clutter shows up so that you can relate to it differently and mitigate its impact on yourself, others, and the environment at large.

What has become clearer to you since you started this book? How have your views on clutter and clearing changed?

Explore

- What has become more clear to me . . .
- Some of the ways that my views on clutter and clearing have changed . . .

WEEK 20
DISSOLVING THE
ILLUSION OF SEPARATION

It was then, while staring out the window, that Ed experienced the strangest feeling he would ever have: a feeling of connectedness, as if all the planets and all the people of all time were attached by some invisible web . . . Everything he'd been taught about the universe and the separateness of people and things felt wrong . . . This wasn't something he was simply comprehending in his mind, but an overwhelmingly visceral feeling, as though he were physically extending out of the window to the very furthest reaches of the cosmos . . . In a single instant, Ed Mitchell had discovered and felt The Force.

—Astronaut Ed Mitchell's account of his Apollo 14 mission to the moon, as recounted by Lynne McTaggart

DAY 134
LOVE MORE, WORRY LESS

A thought popped into my head as I was getting out of bed this morning: "The more you love yourself, the less you'll worry about what people think."

I don't know what inspired it to show up, but it might have had something to do with a recent visit to my parents' house who, at eighty-plus years, continue to have very strong opinions about life (read: politics); ideas that in the past have turned me into a prickly pretzel of unease and resistance.

Not this trip, though. This time, I noticed myself getting less plugged in and riled up, and having more fun enjoying and appreciating my parents just as they are.

Big shift.

I think I'm growing up.

Since most of what we humans think or believe is a form of perception after all—coming through the unique filtering we've constructed from our past experiences—why give up our power and energy to feed someone else's belief or worry when it doesn't feel good to us?

This topic reminds me of a quote I've heard a lot: "What people think of you is none of your business."

Yes, I know, another belief. But one that might help to ease the pressure and create some space.

Explore

- Ways that I still worry about what other people think . . .

- Ways that I no longer worry about what other people think . . .

DAY 135
SHINE YOUR LIGHT BRIGHTLY

This week we're going to dive a little deeper into some ancient spiritual concepts and scientific theory to enhance the context of our clearing. I won't go too off-road, I promise.

The *Rig-Veda* is an ancient religious work of about two hundred and fifty hymns to Lord Indra, the king of the gods in Indian mythology. Indra's Net—the web of life that has at every juncture a jewel that reflects all other jewels—is a useful metaphor for the interconnection of all life in the universe, including universal structures like the Internet. This Eastern model predates the Internet by over 3,500 years!

There appear to be several paraphrased versions of the hymn itself. This one from Frank Joseph's book *Synchronicity & You* is my favorite:

> There is an endless net of threads throughout the universe. The horizontal threads are in space. The vertical threads are in time. At every crossing of the threads, there is an individual. And every individual is a crystal bead. . . . And every crystal bead reflects not only the light from every other crystal in the net, but also every other reflection throughout the entire universe.

In his essay "Approaching Timewave Zero: Part I," Terence McKenna describes what this cosmic web might look like in real terms:

> One way of thinking about it is to compare it to one of those mirrored disco balls, which sends out thousands of reflections off of everybody and everything in the room. The mirrored disco ball is the transcendental object at the end of time, and those reflected twinkling, refractive lights are religions, scientific theories, gurus, works of art, poetry, great orgasms, great souffles, great paintings, etc. Anything that has, in Nietszche's phrase, the "spark of divinity within it," is in fact, referent to the original force of the spark of all divinity unfolding itself within the confines of three-dimensional space.

The bottom line, as I see it, is this: When you shine your light more brightly, you bring everyone else's up with you. Sweet, huh?

Today, notice what happens to those around you when you smile more, laugh more, and feel more at ease. Consider it the "disco ball" in action—beaming *your* light out into the world.

Explore

- When I turn up my light "in here," I notice the world "out there" seems . . .

- It feels good to turn up my light because . . . (Notice the part that is skeptical or cynical.)

DAY 136
THERE IS NO SEPARATION

The implications of an infinitely expandable, cosmic net that unites us all can be rather challenging to our limited self-concept. The idea that we are fundamentally not separate from each other—no "us and them," no "in here, out there"—can be mind-bending.

Imagine not being separate from your home, your neighbors, the people in the next town over, or the next state, or the next continent. Imagine not being separate from the things that press your buttons, your worst enemies, or your clutter! Try, even just for a moment, to imagine these as a reflection and extension of your self.

Allow this concept of no separation to drop into your awareness today.

Explore

- How I know we are not separate from one another . . . (Name and feel the part that isn't so sure.)

- Why I know we are not separate . . .

DAY 137
PARTICIPATORY RELATIONSHIP

Participatory relationship. These two words from Lynne McTaggart's very readable book *The Field* are keys to explaining how the mind works as a powerful manifesting machine.

In quantum physics, "participatory relationship" suggests that a potential something (atomic wave) becomes an actual something (atomic particle) when the thing is *observed*!

For example, a table doesn't materialize out of the ether in isolation just because. It manifests only as it is imagined, observed, and intended. A chair, a car, a meal, a job, a parking space, a *clear home*—these become form because we have given them our attention, our life force, our energy. They wouldn't exist without some degree of conscious or unconscious participation.

This also makes me think of something Dr. Wayne Dyer said in his book, *Being in Balance*: "You get what you think about, whether you want it or not."

What are you giving your attention to? Spend today noticing your thoughts. Are they generally upbeat and positive? Or do they veer into negativity, worry, or fear? Do you make assumptions without checking to see if they're true?

Today, simply notice your thoughts, without judging them as good or bad.

Explore

- I'm giving my attention to . . .
- When I study my thoughts, I notice . . .

DAY 138
NOTICE SYNCHRONICITIES

Last night I dreamt that I had a black dog named Penny. As I was telling my neighbor about it today, you can imagine my surprise when she said that *she* once had a black dog named Penny! What are the chances of that?

It is breathtaking to think that all that we perceive "out there"—outside ourselves—is somehow intricately connected to us. Quantum theory would suggest that the world as we see it—famine and feast, illness and health, war and peace, the Red Sox winning the World Series after eighty-six years—is implicitly shaped by our level of collective consciousness. Yes, even if these events are happening in some remote part of the planet far from where we are!

Spend today noticing synchronicities. Have you run into someone you were thinking about just moments before, for example? Does something you've been hoping for or dreaming about suddenly present itself as an actual possibility? In what ways have your intentions manifested more powerfully since you started working with this book?

Explore
- I've noticed these synchronicities showing up in my life . . .
- My intentions have manifested more powerfully in these ways . . .

DAY 139
WE ARE THEY, THEY ARE US

I don't know if ebola will ever go away. At this writing, it hasn't. Following this week's exploration of no separation, consider this excerpt from Seth Godin's blog:

It starts with, "We" don't have Ebola, "they" do. They live somewhere else, or look different or speak another language. Our kneejerk reaction is that "they" need to be isolated from us . . .

The world is porous, there are more connections than ever, and we've seen this before.

Tuberculosis. Polio. AIDS. Fear runs rampant, amplified by the media, a rising cycle of misinformation, demonization and panic. Fear of the other. Pushing us apart and paralyzing us.

The thing is:

We are they.

They are us.

The work of uncovering the shimmering truth that lies beneath all our stress and stuff may not be easy or pretty for us humans, but it is simple. When we clear one thing or thought with spacious detachment, we can—one baby step at a time—change the world.

Explore

- Recognizing that we are not separate from one another makes me want to . . .
- When I see the world "out there" in pain, I feel . . . (Notice the impulse to "fix" situations outside of yourself in order to quiet—and cover up—the situations that have not been loved and healed within.)

DAY 140
CHECK IN—DISSOLVING
THE ILLUSION OF SEPARATION

The focus this week was to show that we are way bigger and more powerful than we know. The *Rig-Veda* gives us a way to understand how we human beings are not just separate entities cruising along the highway of life, but rather are part of a ginormous cosmic net bound together as one collective manifesting body. It teaches, in essence, that what you do affects me, and what I do affects you. There is no separation. Quantum theory gives us a way to understand how thought becomes form and shows us that where the mind goes energy flows.

What are some of the ways you have felt more perceptive, connected, and/or part of a larger fabric? In what ways do you still believe you are separate from the world "out there"?

If you have not had any big revelations yet, give it time. And keep clearing. One of these days you'll notice yourself experiencing greater flow, opportunities, and magical moments. You're just getting started!

Explore

- Some of the ways I feel more perceptive and connected . . .

- Ways that I believe I am separate . . .

- Magical moments that I've experienced (or hope to experience) . . .

WEEK 21
TAMING
THE MONKEY MIND

I try to quiet the drunken Russian separatists of my own mind
... I pray. I meditate. I rest, as a spiritual act. I spring for organic
cherries. I return phone calls.
—Anne Lamott

DAY 141
MONKEY MIND

It was the Buddha who said that the human mind is like a roomful of
screeching, grasping, drunken monkeys all clamoring to be heard. I like
using the term "monkey mind" to describe that noisy, unsettled, graspy,
fearful, complicating, attached, fidgety, resisting, plugged-in, unspacious part of us that keeps us stuck.

Monkey mind is like a toddler going after the kitchen knife or running into traffic. Reeling it in requires constant attention and infinite
patience—especially when the monkey doesn't like being told "no!"

Next time your mind throws a fit because you're putting a stop to
its tiresome drivel, take a step back and breathe. Watch the resisting
patterns arise. When you give your monkey mind as much space as you
can, you may find it calm down before your eyes.

Explore
- My monkey mind shows up in these ways . . .
- This really gets the monkey going . . .

DAY 142
STRIKE THAT

How do we stop the unsavory chatter that pours out of our heads on a continual basis? How do we keep the noisy stuff from taking over our lives?

You could try the nifty phrase I learned while serving on jury duty. You've probably heard it a lot on TV, if not in an actual courtroom; it's that staccato-like phrase inserted at the end of almost every sentence: *Strike that.*

Every time you catch yourself in monkey mind today, notice if it helps to repeat the phrase *Strike that* to snap you out of la-la land. If that phrase doesn't do it for you, choose a snappier one that does.

Explore
- A word or phrase that helps snap me out of monkey mind is . . .
- When I say it out loud, it feels . . .

DAY 143
ZIP IT, ZAP IT

Stopping a mind that thrives on drama and is stuck on a default setting of doom and gloom takes awareness, and lots of practice. Here's some of the stringy stuff I've been known to chew on over the years—and what detaching from it looks like:

Aghhh . . . the traffic is terrible! We're going to be late to the airport, we're going to miss our plane, our vacation is shot . . . **Strike that.**

Ugh . . . this task is taking forever. I'll never finish clearing my piles . . . it's time to check my emails . . . **Strike that.**

Groan . . . I have no time, there's no food in the fridge, the house feels cold, I'm fried, this day has gone from bad to worse . . . **Strike that.**

What you don't see, but is key to this practice, is me acknowledging and feeling the tightness around my shoulders; noticing that my breathing is halting and shallow; feeling in total resistance, afraid to make a mistake, hungry and running on vapors because I haven't eaten all day and didn't get much sleep the night before.

What unsupportive thoughts can you zap today? . . . Or even right this second?

Explore

- Thoughts I can zap today . . .
- Thoughts I can zap right now . . .

DAY 144
NOT ALLOWED

"When you confronted the victim . . . strike that. When you saw the man with the knife . . . strike that . . ." Courtroom instructions like these can prove challenging for a juror. I mean, seriously, unless you've been lobotomized, erasing a highly charged thought that has made its way into your headspace is not exactly the easiest thing to do.

My experience shows that powerful words create powerful images. And powerful images have a way of sticking like Velcro to anything or anyone that moves. How does one simply ignore a comment that carries tremendous charge?

Easy. You just. don't. go. there.

Just like a courtroom judge instructs, "Nope, can't use it. Not allowed."

Today, notice what your monkey mind does when you say "no" or "stop it!" Allow the queasy, tantrum-y impulses to simply be.

Explore
- Telling my monkey mind to "stop it!" feels . . .
- It is easy (or not so easy) to stop the mental noise because . . .

DAY 145
LEAVE IT!

We all get stuck on something. Today's terrific tip on getting unstuck is courtesy of another one of my students in my online course (thank you, Jim W.!):

> The one sentence I use when I feel attachment coming on is "Leave it!" A dog trainer taught me to say that to my dog a couple years ago. It's what I tell her when we go walking and she gets stuck on something, but I sometimes forget that it works for me too.

Try it: Next time the monkey mind starts grasping (or screeching), gently pull the imaginary leash and firmly say, *Leave it!*

And notice what happens.

Explore
- What happens when I say, "Leave it!" . . .
- What works best to stop the noise in my mind . . .

DAY 146
EFFORT NOT REQUIRED

If you're trying too hard to experience freedom and joy, it's probably because you got stuck on the wrong channel.

As Abraham-Hicks wisely suggests,

> You cannot struggle to joy. Struggle and joy are not on the same channel. You joy your way to joy. You laugh your way to success. It is through your joy that good things come.

Notice the ways that you try harder than you should to be joyful. What can you do to change the channel on your experience?

Explore
- Ways that I struggle to joy . . .
- I can switch to the joy channel by . . .

DAY 147
CHECK IN—
TAMING THE MONKEY MIND

The focus this week was to use simple tools to mind the mind games and change the proverbial channel.

What are some of the games your mind plays? What has helped you mind (and mine) them?

Explore

- Some of the games my mind plays . . .
- What has helped me recognize and stop the mind games this week . . .

WEEK 22
CULTIVATING EASE

Surrender to what is. Say "yes" to life—and see how life suddenly starts working for you rather than against you.
—Eckhart Tolle, *The Power of Now*

DAY 148
IN THE FLOW

Last year, while I was in Mexico, I did something completely out of character for my introverted, worker-bee self.

My Mexican cousin and his posse of ten friends from Mexico City were in town for the weekend. I bumped into them on the street, and like a little tornado of joy they scooped me up and took me to lunch. Only this lunch lasted five hours, and moved on to dinner—at another restaurant outside of town. Our day together went from 1:30 to 11:30 p.m.

We laughed the entire time.

When was the last time you sat with a group of people, eating, schmoozing, and not caring what time it was or what was on the agenda?

If you're thinking prom night, it's been too long.

Explore
- Last time I experienced total ease and joy was . . .
- It is easy (or not easy) for me to go with the flow because . . .

DAY 149
CHOOSE EASE

If I had to choose one phrase from my clearing toolkit that works wonders to quiet the noisy mind and calm the nervous system, it would be this: "I choose ease."

Just saying it slowly seems to have magical powers. The phrase cuts right through stress, jangliness, crankiness, and fatigue, especially if you imagine yourself receiving the phrase like a sponge soaking up water.

Try saying it out loud and watch what happens.

I . . .

choose . . .

ease.

Explore
- When I repeat the phrase "I choose ease" out loud, I feel . . .
- One thing I can do today to invite greater ease is . . .

DAY 150
EASE MEDITATION

Today, I invite you to play with ease by practicing the following steps:

1. **Close your eyes,** and take a deep breath in and a slow, emptying breath out.
2. When you feel centered, *s-l-o-w-l-y* **repeat** the phrase, "I choose ease" on every outbreath for one minute.
3. **Receive** the essential nutrients of this phrase, like a sponge soaking up water.

4. **Repeat** the phrase even—and especially—if your life doesn't feel very easy right now. Every time the mind pipes in with its litany of reasons why ease is not possible, say it again. And again.

5. When you feel ready, **open your eyes** and look around. Notice how you feel.

How does the world respond to you when you're calm?

Explore

- Some ways I can cultivate more ease in my life are . . .

- When I'm calm, the world responds with . . .

DAY 151
NOT ALL CLEARING IS THE SAME

As I see it, there is clearing and there is *clearing*.

There is the old paradigm of clearing clutter that makes us feel bad when we fail and sets us up for disappointment, again and again.

And there's another way, a simpler way, that is infinitely more forgiving and sustainable; a new paradigm that takes the long view and makes us feel capable and good no matter how small the effort.

For us to release the stress and stuff we've been carrying forever, we need to shift our mindset away from the idea of effort and struggle. For clearing to be fun and lasting, we need to undo the notion that we need to "do."

You cannot *will* yourself into a state of ease.

Sit back and be receptive today. If you don't know how, ask your higher self to show you.

Explore
- When I stop efforting, I feel . . .
- What happens when I stop trying so hard . . .
- What I can do today to be more receptive . . .

DAY 152
DEAR ONE, EASE UP

If ease does not come easily to you (and even if it does), you might appreciate this short piece by bestselling author Elizabeth Gilbert, excerpted from a free e-book compilation by Seth Godin called *What Matters Now*:

> Dear ones, EASE UP. Pump the brakes. Take a step back. Seriously. Take two steps back. Turn off all your electronics and surrender over all your aspirations and do absolutely nothing for a spell . . .
>
> Consider actually exhaling. Find a body of water and float. Hit a tennis ball against a wall. Tell your colleagues that you're off meditating (people take meditation seriously, so you'll be absolved from guilt) and then actually, secretly, nap.
>
> My radical suggestion? Cease participation, if only for one day this year—if only to make sure that we don't lose forever the rare and vanishing human talent of appreciating ease.

What is one thing you can "not do" right now to invite greater ease? Notice what it feels like to *consciously* not do.

Explore

- One thing I can "not do" for one minute right now is . . .
- What it feels like to consciously not do . . .

DAY 153
EMERGENCE(Y)

Thanks to Mother Nature and major flooding in our area one year, our basement took a pretty big hit. It was an ugly, exhausting three weeks of drying out, digging out, and extreme clearing that I wouldn't wish on anyone.

We may cultivate easeful non-effort 'til the cows come home, but what happens when we're faced with a crisis? What happens when taking action is critical?

There is no question that action is needed. But action has an even greater impact when it is bolstered by intention, non-identification, and compassion. These Four Pathways of Clearing work as a team. Your team.

This is where your slow-drip practices in awareness, compassionate detachment, and self-care become a lifeline. All those opportunities to clear in baby steps are working to grow your spacious muscle so that when you're thrown a nasty curve ball you'll be ready. You'll be able to embrace anything that comes your way with equanimity.

Explore

- A crisis that I've had to face is . . .
- I handled this crisis by . . .
- I know I'll be able to embrace anything that comes my way because . . .

DAY 154
CHECK IN—CULTIVATING EASE

The focus this week was to cultivate some of clearing's most essential nutrients of non-efforting: ease and receptivity. Adopting a daily clearing practice that incorporates the Four Pathways of Clearing—intention, action, non-identification, and compassion—helps to grow our spacious muscle and balances doing with non-doing.

How does ease show up in your life? Why is it safe to put forth less effort?

Explore
- Ways that ease shows up in my life . . .
- It is safe for me to "effort less" because . . .

WEEK 23
TENDING THE HOME

The tidiest home in the world does not guarantee me a peaceful mind. It is my responsibility to hold myself gently at those times in which nothing feels right at all . . . and look back on all the small steps of progress that have led here.
—Marti S.

DAY 155
PET PEEVES

Here's something that mystifies me: piling a layer of wet dishes on top of a drainer full of dry dishes instead of putting away the original set. Am I the only one who feels this way?

This is not about blame, mind you. I know I have my own share of unconscious behaviors that drive people nuts. But the wet-on-top-of-dry thing just doesn't make sense. It's like taking the clean laundry out of the dryer and throwing it back into the washing machine.

How would it be if everyone on the planet took just one minute to consciously tend to one thing, pile, or area at home every day? Beginning with us here, right now.

Try it: Tune in to one of your housekeeping frustrations for one minute. Notice your resisting behaviors. Once you've zeroed in, ask your higher self to reveal a creative solution that will address the situation and reduce the charge.

PS If my message peeved you today, what can you do to reduce the charge? That would be a good place to start (*wink*).

Explore

- One of my housekeeping pet peeves is . . .
- Tuning in to it feels . . .
- A creative solution that addresses the problem (calms the frustration) is . . .

DAY 156
HOME TENDING MAGIC

Putting things away is one of those ordinary tasks that most of us do without much thought. I know that for some of you, tasks like folding the laundry, washing the dishes, or taking out the trash is a hassle that takes up precious time from other necessities. Like sleep.

What if I told you that daily tending and putting away can be one of the most delicious experiences you can cultivate in the home, a daily practice you'll even come to crave?

Consider today what it might feel like to be enlivened and nourished by housekeeping tasks that you "have to do," or do on autopilot. Hold a space for that as a possibility.

Can you feel the energy shifting (or rising) by simply reading these words? (If they bring up feelings of annoyance or any other reaction, your practice today is to give these resisting patterns some space.)

Explore

- Housekeeping tasks that give me no pleasure . . .
- What it might feel like to be enlivened and nourished by them . . .

DAY 157
HOUSEKEEPING HEALS

Yes! Housekeeping heals. Putting away every day feels good. Mindful tending has a way of growing your sense of ease and well-being.

Don't take my word for it. These truths need to be lived and practiced for them to be fully realized.

Try it: Take a moment to look away from this book. Do you see anything that is out of place? If so, take one minute to put it away. With awareness.

Tend. Be Mindful. Repeat . . .

Explore
- Something that is out of place right now . . .
- What it feels like to put it away with awareness . . .

DAY 158
FIND A HOME AND PUT IT AWAY

Possessions not having a home or not being put away is much more than a housekeeping issue. It reflects a level of unconsciousness and neglect that can easily be remedied. As Gunilla Norris writes in her fabulous book, *Being Home*, "How we hold simplest of our tasks speaks loudly about how we hold life itself."

What is one thing that has no home and/or never gets put away on a regular basis? It could be your car keys, loose change, credit card receipts . . . If nothing comes to mind, consider taking another virtual tour of your home and having another heart-to-heart chat with her (see Day 81).

Explore

- One thing that has no home (and/or never gets put away) is . . .
- What it feels like . . .
- One thing I can do today to change that is . . .

DAY 159
AMAZING IN THE ORDINARY

I love it when readers and students write in to tell me how clearing is changing their lives. It is comments like these that make it all worth it, like this one from Lesly:

> I've had a real insight today. I realize that I do not pay attention when I put things away. I psychologically detach myself from doing something else more interesting. To my surprise, when I focus my awareness on placing an object carefully in its home, I get pleasure from that. Applying awareness to what I'm doing, yes, even if it is clearing up—boring clearing up—gives me pleasure. How amazing.

There are infinite ways to insert awareness into ordinary tasks and move stuck energy. Here are some of my favorites:

- Make the bed
- Push chairs in after a meal
- Turn off the lights
- Cap the toothpaste
- Lower the toilet seat
- Fluff up the sofa pillows

All you need is sixty seconds a day to grow a new habit. What new habits would you like to grow?

Explore
- New habits that I would like to grow . . .
- Ways that simple daily home tending has nourished me . . . (and surprised me . . .)

DAY 160
H-OM-E

It might not look like much initially, but there is a powerful ripple effect that happens when we tend our homes.

Spend some time today reflecting on the clearing ripple effect: How are your new housekeeping habits affecting other members of your family? How are they rippling into other areas of your life?

Not to sound like a broken record, but there is no separation. Your clearing is my clearing. Your clearing is everybody's clearing.

Explore
- How my home tending is affecting my house . . .
- How my home tending is affecting my life . . .
- How my home tending is affecting others . . .

DAY 161
CHECK IN—TENDING THE HOME

The focus this week was to experience home tending as a pathway to well-being: to transform a potentially mindless, utilitarian housekeeping task into a mindful, sacred practice that can lift, lighten, and illuminate us all.

Did you have any aha moments this week from tending to your home or putting things away? Were any of the lessons difficult or annoying to you?

With a monkey mind in constant hover mode, it bears repeating this simple truth: Clearing is not about completing a task; it is about how you *relate* to the task. Allowing all of your resisting patterns to arise without doing anything to fix or manage them is where the real magic is, where the true clearing happens.

Explore
- Finding a home for my things and putting them away regularly feels . . .
- What still (no longer) pisses me off . . .
- Aha moments that I've experienced this week . . .

WEEK 24
EASING PAIN

Pain is not the same as suffering. Left to itself, the body discharges pain spontaneously, letting go of it the moment that the underlying cause is healed. Suffering is pain that we hold on to. It comes from the mind's mysterious instinct to believe that pain is good, or that it cannot be escaped, or that the person deserves it.

—Deepak Chopra, *The Book of Secrets*

DAY 162
EXPANDING AND CONTRACTING

I remember when Hurricane Sandy delivered a massive punch to all of us on the East Coast. With the winds gusting upward of eighty miles an hour, amazingly, our home did not lose power, our basement stayed dry, and no trees fell down. We were the lucky ones.

That said, this storm affected me deeply. For days before the storm hit I felt out of sorts. I was having wild dreams. My lower back hurt. My body ached. I felt nauseous. I could tell something big was about to blow . . . unhinge . . . release.

Whether you too ended up on the lucky side of Sandy's wrath or not, the truth is, this was a massive space clearing for all of us here on the planet. Sometimes it takes a gigantic, real-life hurricane (tornado, fire, flood) to move us—to lift us out of our coma and clear out what isn't working in our lives.

Birthing hurts sometimes.

What's brewing in your life right now? What are you ready to move through to birth?

Explore
- Something I can feel is wanting to be born . . .
- Gentle steps I can take to make it more real . . .

DAY 163
PAIN IS ENERGY

We have all experienced physical pain. It is part of our human condition. Like with everything we've been talking about in this book, pain is a form of energy too—wave patterns that form, un-form, and in-form.

If pain is energy, isn't it true then that we can work with pain by following the same Four Pathways of Clearing—intention, action, non-identification, and compassion—to ease its disturbing effects?

We'll spend the next two weeks exploring this question. Be gentle with yourself.

Explore
- How physical pain tends to show up in my life . . .
- Where in the body I tend to feel this pain . . .

DAY 164
EASE THE PAIN

Practicing non-identification helps us shift from a fixing mode to an observing mode; from willing things to happen to allowing them to happen. There's no better teacher to help us cultivate spacious detachment, I believe, than pain.

I have used my own physical aches and emotional weather as my private laboratory, and it continues to be one of my most valuable teachers.

Because I see pain as a signal of contraction (versus expansion), I want to follow the pain to the tender place from where it came.

To the degree that I am able to enter the hurt or the wound with compassionate awareness, more often than not I find that the pain eases or goes away altogether. This is advanced clearing.

What has worked in the past to help you ease pain—mindfully (not chemically)? Have you ever tried observing the pain and breathing through it before?

Explore

- What has helped me ease pain more mindfully . . .
- When I observe pain without immediately trying to "fix" or medicate it, I notice . . .

DAY 165
PAY ATTENTION INWARD NOW

In my practice of not identifying pain as "my" pain, I've noticed that many garden-variety sensations recede almost as quickly as they come. A muscle spasm in my foot or calf, which has had the effect of bolting me up from the deepest sleep and disabling me with agonizing ferocity, for example, now passes in less than five seconds. Stomachaches and headaches generally pass quickly, too. Using physical sensations to practice detachment—from simple annoyances to unmitigated agony—has been a profound lesson in spacious detachment.

This awareness approach to managing pain did not happen overnight. Neither am I a glutton for punishment. My threshold for physical pain is pretty low, in fact, and I'll be the first to go after the usual medical protocols for pain relief if they are warranted and advised and I just can't stand it anymore.

What I'm suggesting here is that the body offers us an opportunity to go within, pay attention, and feel. Iyanla Vanzant even created a handy acronym for this idea: PAIN = Pay Attention Inward Now.

What ache or pain—physical, mental, emotional, or spiritual—is calling you inside?

Explore

- An ache or pain that has been calling my attention . . .
- When I bring all of my awareness to it without judging it (or myself), I notice . . .

DAY 166
LEAN INTO PAIN

Today, lean into any pains, aches, or heartaches; any impulses to contract, cringe, shut down, push away, space out, digress, interrupt, or tamp down. This is your chance to go deeper—to find the tender part of you and embrace the pattern before the body goes into lockdown mode.

Allow these wise teachings of Pema Chödrön to help you:

Take an interest in your pain and your fear. Move closer, lean in, get curious; even for a moment, experience the feelings without labels, beyond being good or bad. Welcome them. Invite them. Do anything that helps melt the resistance.

A word to the wise: This practice of "being with," or dis-identifying, from pain does not replace the role of health care professionals to diagnose and treat physical or emotional conditions. It is very important to remember that if at any point any symptom or disturbance persists in your journey, you need to pick up the phone and get help!

Explore

- A situation that causes me to hurt (contract, cringe, recoil, shut down, space out, digress, tamp down) . . . (and what it feels like exactly from a sensory perspective . . .)
- When I lean into this energy even more, I notice . . .

DAY 167
CHANGING THE FREQUENCY OF PAIN

On Day 73, I listed **five simple truths about energy**. Here are some of them again, reframed in the context of pain:

1. Humans are like radios: We receive and transmit information as energy all the time.
2. Not everything we feel is ours. The body processes information that it picks up in the ether, and it only becomes "ours" the moment we believe it to be ours.
3. Pain shows us our blocks.
4. Physical pain is a good indicator that we are resisting the natural, free flow of universal energy, or well-being, which is always available to us.
5. Ease feels good; unease (dis-ease) does not.

If pain is energy vibrating at a specific frequency, we can relieve it by changing the frequency. What are you ready to change up today?

Explore
- Pain that I know is not mine . . .

- When I tune in to the contracted frequency of pain and compare it to that of spacious ease, I notice . . .
- What I am ready to change up . . .

DAY 168
CHECK IN—EASING PAIN

This week we saw how pain can be a teacher. It shows us patterns that no longer serve us, and gives us practice leaning into them and letting go. Because pain can be so immediate and unequivocal, it can show us the way out.

How does pain usually show up in your life? Is it physical, mental, emotional, spiritual? All of the above? Do you notice an impulse to numb the pain—with denial, distraction, food, alcohol, drugs, or something else?

Explore
- The kind of pain I tend to experience . . . (and how I deal with it is . . .)
- What pain is teaching me about me . . .
- The way out is . . .

WEEK 25
BREAKING
THE CHAIN OF PAIN

Hurt people hurt people. That's how pain patterns get passed on, generation after generation after generation.

Break the chain today. Meet anger with sympathy, contempt with compassion, cruelty with kindness. Greet grimaces with smiles. Forgive and forget about finding fault.

Love is the weapon of the future.

—Yehuda Berg

DAY 169
HURT PEOPLE HURT PEOPLE

"Hurt people hurt people." That is one terrific memory aid if I've ever seen one. It's a lifeline—with a lot of slack—that can help us move through layers of blame and shame.

And yes, moving through takes work: It takes courage to be vulnerable, to name and feel the tangled mess of hurt, to embrace years of painful buildup and let it all hang out, as one of my online students, Aryel P., so poignantly shares here:

I just got to the lesson [on "Hurt People Hurt People"]—or should I say, it got to me! I felt the tears stream down my face as I journaled and I heard my inner voice, self-talk saying: "Yeah, but . . ." And it says inside me, "Gee, I am sorry about *their* hurt, but did it have to cost me *my* youth and joy; *my* job and reputation? Did it have to break *my* heart? Did *their* hurt and problems have to undo *my* security and life dreams? Did *their* hurt have to hurt *me* so that I would hurt others?

I wipe away the tears and blow my snotty nose and turn to the front of my journal, where I keep my copy of "If" by Rudyard Kipling, and I read it yet again.

Everything is indeed attached.

I feel the walls of my old self crumbling down in a new way. It is as if the cement binding each stone I have put so carefully in place is dissolving, and the stones slowly lose their place in the wall and begin to slip and tumble.

What hurt are you ready to let go of (dissolve) today? What happens when you name and feel it without blame and attachment?

Explore
- A hurt that I'm ready to release today . . . (and what it feels like when I name and feel it completely . . .)
- How I see that my hurt hurts others . . .

DAY 170
IT'S NOT ABOUT YOU

Whenever you feel a rant or shame wave coming on because some-one has offended you, overlooked you, neglected you, challenged you, abused your trust, or even abused you in unthinkable ways . . . guess what? You can shift the energy of attack with this simple four-word reminder: Hurt people hurt people.

The pain that is being flung about is *not about you.*

Explore

- Saying "It's not mine," or "It's not about me" feels . . .
- What can help me remember to be *bigger* than the pain . . .

DAY 171
LOW-FREQUENCY VEILS

As horrible as some people may act sometimes, it helps to remember that their actions are filtered through their own low-frequency veil of hurt, stuckness, and pain.

What is one transgression that you've been holding on to? What would it take to let it go?

Explore

- I'm ready to let go of . . .
- I am bigger than this because . . .

DAY 172
NIP IT IN THE BUD

One of best ways to nip a deep-seeded pattern in the bud begins with you noticing it as soon as it happens, before it takes root. It begins with being (fiercely) vigilant of the thoughts you spin—those fearful, derailing, low-vibrational energetic weapons that not only keep you stuck, but have a way of sticking around.

As Abraham-Hicks so wisely tells us, "Your choices of action may be limited—but your choices of thought are not."

What is one thought you've been spinning around for a while? Now would be a good time to nip it before it leaves a sticky residue. (Keep nipping it until it no longer holds a charge.)

Explore

- A painful thought I have been holding on to and spinning is . . .
- What would help to "nip it" before it does more damage . . .

DAY 173
MIND YOUR OWN BUSINESS

A little mindful detachment repeated over and over again goes a long way in shifting (and lifting) things for everybody—for good.

Can you imagine a world where we are all compassionately minding our own business (as it were), and allowing others to mind theirs?

Explore

- What helps me remember that other people's stories are *not mine* . . .
- One way I can mind my own business today . . .

DAY 174
RELEASE PAINFUL MEMORIES MEDITATION

Today's meditation is designed to release pain from the past. Do it when you have ten minutes to be alone.

1. **Close your eyes,** and take a deep breath in and a slow, emptying breath out.
2. When you feel centered, **recall** a time when someone you care about did or said something deeply hurtful. What

happened? Who was there? Did you react or respond? Did you get small and collapse? Or did you puff up in vengeful or defensive anger? Take a minute to bring up many of the sensations that were true for you that day and notice if they still push a button.

3. **Imagine** all the pain—the physical sensations, mental entanglements, and emotional charge—as a big ball of energy swirling in and around you. Is there a shape, color, smell, or sound associated with this swirling mass?

4. **Allow** this energy to lose its grip on you, and **watch** as it melts away (or evaporates, dissolves, lifts, sloughs off—whatever feels best).

5. **Take a step back** (in your mind's eye, or a real one) and watch the energy ball recede from your personal space until it disappears from your field and diffuses completely.

6. When you see that the energy has disappeared, take a deep breath in and out and **notice how you feel.**

7. **Open your eyes** and write down your experiences in your clearing journal and bookmark it to return to in a month's time. If the ball is still there, repeat the steps above.

Explore

- What the swirling ball of pain looked and felt like . . .
- What it feels like to release pain from my energy field . . .
- How I feel now . . .

DAY 175
CHECK IN—
BREAKING THE CHAIN OF PAIN

In these past two weeks we looked at physical, mental, and emotional pain as energy and a pathway to releasing old patterns.

In what ways have you moved beyond seeing pain as "yours"? Have you noticed that by simply bringing awareness to the pain, it shifts, or melts completely? How do you feel today after yesterday's clearing of a painful memory?

Explore

- I have moved beyond seeing "pain" as mine in these ways . . .
- Inserting compassionate awareness shifts my pain by . . .
- After yesterday's clearing meditation, I feel . . .

WEEK 26
TAKING TIME TO PAUSE

Looking behind I am filled with gratitude.
Looking forward I am filled with vision.
Looking upwards I am filled with strength.
Looking within I discover peace.
— Prayer, Source Unknown

DAY 176
REST STOP

This week marks the halfway point in our journey together. Whether your experience has been one of daily revelations, slow and steady progress, or an interminable slog, I'm here to tell you that you've come a long way.

Yes, we've gone through fog and muck. We've climbed hills. We've moved mountains. Even if it doesn't feel like much has happened.

Take today to put the backpack down, put your feet up, take a sip of water, and look around at where you've landed. What do you see? What are you grateful for?

Remember, you are not alone. We are all in this together.

Explore
- In this moment of pause I can see . . .
- I'm grateful for . . .

DAY 177
GOOD AMNESIA

One of the things I always tell my clients after a consultation is to notice the changes in their life and write them down. This is because the difficulties that prompted them to call me for a session begin to disappear like magic. Yes, disappear. Out of home, out of head, out of life.

Once you've released physical and emotional baggage, it's easy to forget that you were ever burdened. The junk in the garage, the difficult relationship, the bad job, money troubles, a painful past—all will feel like a distant memory, or like they never happened.

It's a good type of amnesia to have. The good memories of your past will always remain intact, while the painful ones will seem irrelevant and begin to melt away.

If you're wondering how that might be so, consider this: When you vibrate at a higher frequency as a result of clearing, those low-frequency energies that used to disturb and define you are no longer supportable.

Raise your frequency and everything will change.

What old habits have become unsupportable in your life? Have you noticed yourself being less interested in engaging in certain activities, or connecting with certain people, or eating foods that don't feel good? Is it easier to move clutter out of the house?

What is starting to fall away from your life? Notice that.

Explore
- I've noticed these things starting to fall away . . .
- Habits (activities, people, foods) that no longer support me . . .

DAY 178
IT'S A JOURNEY

You may have noticed over the past six months that the inner work of clearing can be messy and inscrutable sometimes. You may feel like you haven't made much progress, or you've had days where you just want to go back to snuggling with your old comfortable habits. Maybe you've even fallen off the wagon a few times. What I wrote in *Your Spacious Self* bears mentioning again:

> There is no crash course on how to evolve. You cannot buy clarity and wisdom at the store or manufacture it in a lab or train for it. Life does not always lend itself to being tidied or packaged, and our experiences do not always add up at the end of the day.

Clearing is a journey, not a destination. Even if you don't see the whole picture yet, you have put into motion a powerful new combination of habits that *are working*, though perhaps quietly behind the scenes.

Use today to make a list of what *is* working in your life. Then, choose one thing and focus your attention on it. Allow sensations to arise—including the uncomfortable bits.

Explore
- What is working in my life . . .
- One thing that is working in my life that I can give more energy to . . .

DAY 179
KEEP MOVING

In June 1956, a young Rev. Dr. Martin Luther King spoke at the 47th Annual NAACP Convention in San Francisco in favor of the Montgomery bus boycott. One of the things he said was, "If you can't fly, run; if you can't run, walk; if you can't walk, crawl—but, by all means, keep moving."

Realizing a dream, any dream, can be messy and time-consuming. Whether it is creating good art, clearing out a massively cluttered house, or learning a new skill, the pathway to success can look like a squiggly mess: two steps forward, three back, four sideways, one more forward, and so on.

In the absence of discernible progress, and a wily monkey mind shouting all the reasons why *it will never work*, it is easy to lose hope and cave.

Whatever happens, don't give up. Don't give in to a noisy and attached mind that thinks it knows better (it doesn't). Don't give in to a mind that is regurgitating a tired script of old stories, worries, and memories from the *past*.

The truth is, achieving anything that matters takes work. It takes time to release old habits and grow new ones. It takes time to rewire the brain. It takes time to get good at something.

Never lose hope. There is more going on than meets the eye.

What will help you keep moving forward today? *Do that.* Even if it's just for one minute.

Explore
- One thing that will help me remember not to give up and give in . . .
- What I can do right now to keep moving . . .

DAY 180
CLEARING AS A SPIRITUAL PRACTICE

It's not every day that I see a book or article by someone who makes the same case as I do about clearing as a spiritual practice. So when this piece by Geri Larkin, founder and former head teacher of Still Point Zen Buddhist Temple, came across my desk, I had to share it. Here's an excerpt:

> We have to let go of our stuff.
>
> But we don't, or at least we don't want to. This is a serious spiritual issue, this clinging. We may be able to give up lovers, Facebook friends . . . even our waistlines, but do not, do not, ask us to give up the three photographs taken of us in 1996 when we looked like Kate Moss on a good day . . .
>
> Added up, objects become clutter. Clutter becomes noise. And noise—in all of its forms—blocks spiritual growth, starting with an inability to simply feel happy. Happiness needs quiet. If we watch, we'll feel its presence when we are meditating, watching the sun set, or maybe rocking the almost sleeping baby. The more noise, the harder it is for happiness to show her face.

What are you still clinging to that is making too much noise? What blocks your joy?

Explore
- I am still clinging on to . . .
- What is blocking my joy . . .

DAY 181
TO SHARE OR NOT TO SHARE?

As we continue on our clearing path, let's take a moment to consider the importance of feeling safe. One of my students recently asked this question, and it resonated with many in our class:

Once you identify what you are feeling about a certain person, do you tell them?

The short answer is, not necessarily. Our work on feeling with compassionate awareness is mostly internal. The good news here is that adopting a daily practice of clearing this way increases your chance of healing any relationship (with a person, thing, or issue) without having to say or do anything.

The only "telling" I recommend is sharing your feelings with someone who can hold a witnessing space for you: someone who is not attached to the issue or the outcome, and can listen without giving advice or fixing.

If you're feeling like you could use some extra support at this stage in your journey—a container that your feelings can bump up against in a safe way—it's never too late to ask a good friend or two to join you on this ride. Have him or her read the introduction of this book, complete the first three weeks to understand the principles and get the hang of the practices, and join you on the trail at this or any juncture.

This is a case where more equals more, where joining together and sharing with other big hearts can lighten the load exponentially for everyone!

Explore

- I feel safe sharing my experiences with . . .
- I don't yet feel safe sharing my experiences with . . .

DAY 182
CHECK IN—TAKING TIME TO PAUSE

The focus this week was to pause, take stock, and remember that clearing is a journey, not a race. As the halfway point, this is a good opportunity to reflect on how things are going for you.

Are you feeling more energized than when you started, eager to embrace each new daily reveal? Or are you running out of juice, yo-yoing back and forth between good days and not-so-good days? Remember, you are right where you should be. Progress is not always linear, and acceptance is key throughout this process.

Explore

- Changes I've seen in myself since I began this book . . .
- Ways I feel more (or less) comfortable with the up-and-down nature of clearing . . .
- What would help me stay on track . . .

WEEK 27
RELEASING WITH WATER

You can change the world with a hot bath, if you sink into it from a place of knowing that you are worth profound care, even when you're dirty and rattled. Who knew?
—Anne Lamott, *Small Vctories*

DAY 183
MOVE WITH THE FLOW

Moved by her joyful retrospectives of her contributions to the world, I emailed Oprah Winfrey at the end of her twenty-fifth season. I thanked her for giving us so much, being so real, and inspiring us to embrace more of who we truly are.

It must have put me on a list because I received a lovely reply. (Me and probably millions of others.) With no fancy header at the top, no click-through buttons promoting stuff, no perfect punctuation, I was touched by her genuinely sisterly message about life after Harpo. Here's an excerpt:

> Started out the week taking swimming lessons. Moving beyond my amateur doggy paddle. Learned the breast stroke today. . . .
>
> For years I've been a challenged swimmer, afraid of the water and fighting it. Today I learned to move with the flow.
>
> This I've known forever is the great metaphor of life. "Move with the flow." Don't fight the current.

Resist nothing. Let life carry you. Don't try to carry it.

Sometimes we just have to be reminded. A swim lesson did it for me.

What has helped you learn to move with the flow?

Explore

- What has helped me move with the flow . . .
- What moving with the flow feels like . . .

DAY 184
LIQUID MEMORY AID

Today I invite you to wash your hands to cultivate awareness. Resist the urge to "get it over with" and notice what it feels like when you take your time.

Allow the sight of running water—flowing from the faucets in the sink, shower, bath, laundry, hose . . . to help you remember to . . .

Stop. Breathe. Let go.

Explore

- The impulse to rush and "get it over with" feels . . .
- What it feels like to take my time . . .

DAY 185
SCENTS AND SENSIBILITY

Have you ever wondered how many times a day you wash your hands? Or noticed what it feels like? Are you aware of the water temperature, the quality and smell of the soap you're using, or how long you keep your hands in the water? Do you notice the texture of the towel you use to dry your hands?

Given a choice in a public restroom, do you reach for a paper towel or the hand dryer? Environmental impact notwithstanding, which of these approaches leaves you feeling loved-up and well tended?

Take the time today to wash your hands *slowly*, in a way that honors you. If you have a fabulous, divine-smelling bar of soap, use it.

Take a good, long time to dry your amazing hands, which don't get credit for what they do for us every waking minute.

Ahh . . . How's your breathing now?

Explore
- Washing and honoring my hands in a nourishing way feels . . .
- When I look at my hands, I see . . . (Name and feel any judgments and breathe them out.)

DAY 186
WASH AND RELEASE

Is there something today that is troubling you, keeping you up at night, or making you feel blocked?

If so, there's a Japanese saying that may help: "Let the things of long ago drift away on the water." That is, let bygones be bygones. Today, try using intentional hand washing, bathing, or dish washing to release the charge that is keeping you stuck. Imagine the water washing away all the stressful buildup of whatever is troubling you, while new water flowing from the spigot brings in new energies to cleanse, refresh, and uplift.

There is nothing that you're holding on to that cannot be washed away.

Explore

- Washing my troubles away feels . . .
- It is safe for me to let go of the past because . . .

DAY 187
DRINK UP

Have you ever noticed how thirsty you get after you've been clearing? This is because you are processing a lot of energy.

Drinking lots of good water is space clearing's best friend. It reduces the side effects of clearing and helps you feel better fast.

Next time you consciously clear, put away, or address a difficult situation, notice your thirst and be sure to have a bottle of water on hand before tackling a task.

Bottoms up, everyone!

Explore

- I notice I get really thirsty when . . .
- The last time I had a glass of water was . . .

DAY 188
WASHING MEDITATION

This one-minute washing practice goes hand in hand with the others you've tried this week. It uses intentional breathing as a way to release what's holding you back.

1. **Run your faucet** for a few seconds today until the water temperature feels just right.
2. **Fill the sink** with water.
3. **Breathe in** *ease* as you watch the water level rise.
4. **Place your hands** in the bowl and wash them slowly for one minute, breathing normally.
5. **Breathe out** slowly with the word *r-e-l-e-a-s-e* as you empty the bowl.

Explore
- Breathing in ease feels . . .
- Breathing out release feels . . .

DAY 189
CHECK IN—RELEASING WITH WATER

The focus this week was to use the gentle flow of water to release stuck energy and anchor an experience in letting go.

In what ways has intentional washing and bathing helped to create more flow in your life? In what ways has taking your time, honoring your hands, and drinking more water made you feel nourished this week?

Explore

- Ways that I've noticed water helping me move stuck energy and create more flow . . .

- Ways that I feel nourished from these experiences . . .

WEEK 28
LETTING IN
THE LIGHT

You are just a few laughs from letting a whole lot of good stuff in.

You are just a few kisses from letting a whole lot of good stuff in.

You are just a little bit of relief from letting a whole lot of good stuff in.

—Abraham-Hicks

DAY 190
WHAT CLEARING CAN
LOOK AND FEEL LIKE

Do you ever have those special-occasion days that end up unraveling into an emotional heap?

It was a beautiful Thanksgiving Day last year, and we were thrilled to have our daughter home with us. With dinner plans scheduled for later on, the day was wide open to have some feel-good time as a family.

Didn't happen.

We couldn't find our groove. We spent most of the day orbiting around each other in separate worlds: my husband going for a run, our daughter writing on her laptop, me working hard to meet a deadline for an online course I was creating. When I was ready to go for our walk, my daughter was out running, and my husband was taking a nap.

Seems benign, until you start to throw in expectation, disappointment, hunger, discord, impatience—the "perfect storm" conditions (in my case) for old abandonment issues to rear their ugly little head. Yes, my buttons got royally pushed on that Thanksgiving Day.

What made this perfect storm different, though, was that I was able to process the emotional weather the moment I became aware of it. Instead of letting the poor-me patterns fester like they used to in the old days, I closed my eyes and went inside to the place that hurt the most: my heart space. What I felt and saw with my mind's eye was a dark, gucky, chaotic energy swirling around an image of the three of us facing outward, completely disconnected from one another. Beneath all that was a wave of deep, amorphous grief.

So I watched and felt and allowed my squirmy self to not like it at all. I watched my impulses to bolt and disappear and make everyone feel really bad. I witnessed the gucky energy. I felt the gucky energy. I inserted as much compassionate awareness as I could into that gucky energy.

For about five minutes I observed and allowed. I became my own witnessing presence.

Over the course of about fifteen minutes, I watched as the area around my heart space began to grow lighter, brighter, and clearer. My nervous system had calmed. I felt restored. I felt myself again. When I opened my eyes, I felt strangely cleansed and purified.

And the other best part is that my family seemed lighter, brighter, and clearer too.

Explore

- This situation from my past has brought up an old wound . . . (what it looked and felt like . . .)
- When I insert compassionate awareness into the wound, I can feel . . .

DAY 191
RECEIVE WITH SIMPLICITY

Rashi, a medieval French rabbi and author, advises, "Receive with simplicity everything that happens to you."

You could also receive things the hard way. But why would you want to?

Good question. Back in the day when our daughter was in elementary school, I remember how hard I made things for myself (and others) by insisting that I take on the get-ready-for-school detail. For two non–morning people, let's just say the daily wrangles over waking up, getting dressed, and making lunch were far from harmonious.

When my husband took over the morning routine (out of sheer desire for peace and quiet in our household), I still couldn't let go of my need to be in charge. I couldn't receive the simplicity of what was being offered to me. I mean really. Who cares if the hair is not parted perfectly and the socks don't match? I can laugh about it now, but I cringe at the thought of how long it took me to surrender; to *give it a friggin' rest!*

Do you notice situations where you tend to make things more difficult for yourself? Use today to notice them *and* the offerings of support that seem to magically appear to make your life easier.

What are you ready to receive the easy way?

Explore

- Situations in which I tend to make things more difficult for myself . . .

- What I'm ready to receive the easy way . . .

- What I can let go of to receive it . . .

DAY 192
IT'S NOT PERSONAL

We've talked quite a bit about how certain spaces can make us feel drained, enervated, or wiped out. The world is full of low-vibrational frequencies swirling in the ether. And it's very easy to get sideswiped by them when we're not paying attention.

When was the last time you got derailed by someone or something? Are you able to recognize that anything that doesn't feel good does not have to be "yours"?

Explore

- An energy that threw me off recently was . . .
- This energy made me feel . . .
- I know it wasn't mine because . . .

DAY 193
SHINING LIGHT

Scroll down the following statements and check those that apply to you. Nothing to "do" but notice the ones that elicit the slightest pang (gulp, eye roll, snicker) of unease:

- I still have clothes in my closet that don't fit.
- My handbag is still a mess.
- I still have tolerations that I can't seem to get to.
- I've had projects for years that I have yet to finish.
- I run endless-loop tapes in my head that begin with "I should."

- I'm ashamed to let anyone see my home.
- I'm afraid to slow down.
- I need help but am afraid to ask for it.
- I feel guilty when I take time to do something for myself.
- I let people down when I make mistakes.

Which statements hit a nerve? Can you allow your buttons to get pressed without beating yourself up? What would help you feel compassionate self-acceptance?

Explore
- The statements that hit a nerve . . .
- What would help me accept and allow my flaws . . .

DAY 194
LET IN THE GOOD STUFF

Can you feel it?

If you really stop and tune in for a second, can you feel the "good stuff" bubbling and forming just below the gucky stuff?

It's right there, just waiting for you to discover, experience, and embrace it.

What will it take for you to uncover it?

If you don't know, ask your higher self to show you in ways that you will readily recognize and feel.

Explore
- Just beneath the discomfort I can feel . . .
- When I ask my higher self to show me answers, and wait for them, I notice . . .

DAY 195
MAKE LIGHT WORK

You don't need any tools to create a joyous, spacious, clutter-free life besides this amazing package we call the human body and this elastic generator we call the mind.

In the end, clearing is working with light. We are light workers in this way:

- We **shine** light by being a witness.
- We **receive** light by being vulnerable.
- We **become** light when we bring the two together.

What does light mean to you?

Explore
- I feel light when . . .
- When I am light, I notice . . .

DAY 196
CHECK IN—LETTING IN THE LIGHT

The focus this week was to play with energy a bit more, exploring different frequencies of light and offering up examples of how we might clear a difficult situation and make life a little bit easier for ourselves.

In what ways do you feel lighter, brighter, or clearer this week? In what ways have you become more of a witnessing presence in your life?

Explore

- Ways that I feel lighter, brighter, or clearer this week . . .
- I've been able to witness more of (and react less to) . . .

WEEK 29
BEING BOLD, BEING VULNERABLE

Courage starts with showing up and letting ourselves be seen.
—Brené Brown, *Daring Greatly*

DAY 197
QUEASY VULNERABILITY

Last year I was invited to give some talks in the Netherlands as part of the Dutch release of my first book. How could I say no? It sounded so fun.

It wasn't until I was on the plane hurtling across the Atlantic that the doubts began to fly. *Will my workshop design work for this audience? Will my contact recognize me at the airport? Do I have to dial the country code if I'm already in the country?*

A large knot of fear began to form in my belly as I headed to a place I had never been, into the hands of people I had never met, to teach audiences who might not get me or my message.

Stop. This. Plane!

From all my years of clearing (and traveling), you'd think I'd remember that something always happens when you deliberately step into that messy netherworld of not knowing. What happens is vulnerability—that quivery, queasy wave of energy that strips you to the bone and exposes everything.

What also happens is magic—that thrilling rush that comes when you open yourself up to the boundless love and support that is out there, just waiting to rush in when you soften your grip of attachment long enough to receive it.

Explore

- A time when I felt vulnerable . . .
- What vulnerability feels like to me (as energy) . . .

DAY 198
IT TAKES COURAGE TO LET GO

In one of my workshop retreats, we spend two and a half days embracing the myriad ways we hold on, both excruciating and comical. We talk about how our stress and stuff makes us feel. Then, we release it ceremonially with love.

Here's an excerpt of one of my blog posts about the effect of this exercise:

> One person's pledge to delete the 4,000 emails from 2009 was met with a collective gasp. Our clammy hands clapped enthusiastically to her resolve and courage. Another talked about how he was going to change his answering machine message to "If your call is important to me, I will return it." For a third it took everything she had to simply breathe more deeply.
>
> It takes courage to really let go. It takes courage to feel the feelings that come up when you take a decisive step and face your fears. It takes courage to commit to what really matters.
>
> Courage—as in "heart"—if you go by the original meaning of the word.

If you were to pledge to do something that is outside of your comfort zone, what would it be? What would en-courage you to take that step? Remember, it doesn't have to be dramatic or crazy big. Any one baby step you take with awareness that moves stuck energy is courageous.

Explore
- One thing I'm ready to do (let go of) that is a stretch . . .
- What encourages me to take that step . . .

DAY 199
LIVE WHOLEHEARTEDLY

In her 2010 TED talk "The Power of Vulnerability," social work researcher Brené Brown shares the story of how she came to understand what separates those who live wholeheartedly—that is, those who have a strong sense of worthiness, love, and sense of belonging—from those who struggle for it. She suggests that if we want true connection to happen with another person, we have to allow ourselves to be seen. Really seen.

In what ways are you allowing yourself to really be seen (or not)? What would help you feel safe to come out of hiding?

Explore
- What happens when I allow myself to be really seen . . . (and what scares me is . . .)
- What would help me feel safe to come out of hiding . . .

DAY 200
LEAN INTO FEAR

What is one thing that scares you? Go with your first impulse. Keep it simple. Choose something that doesn't overwhelm or fry your circuits. Allow any discomfort to arise to the degree that you can handle it.

There. How bad was that? Is it possible to lean into the discomfort of it just a teeny bit? And breathe?

Repeat the process every day and watch the resisting patterns begin to dissolve.

Explore
- One thing that scares me right now . . .
- Leaning into the fear feels . . .

DAY 201
TELL THE TRUTH

The way I see it, just closing your eyes, diving into a task, and hoping for the best is not going to cut it.

For clearing to be sustainable, you need to take measured (baby) steps to bypass the fear response.

You also need to tell the truth about your experience. When you add conscious awareness to your courage, you create space to feel.

Explore
- What is true for me right now . . .
- One baby step I can take today to face a truth I've been avoiding is . . .

DAY 202
WHY YOU MATTER

While we're on the subject of truth telling, notice what happens when you breathe in and complete the phrase, "Why I matter . . ."

Try it: Sit in quiet contemplation for a few minutes and allow all thoughts and sensations to arise. Notice and allow all the squirmy bits to come up too.

When you allow yourself to drop into the truth of why you exist and why you matter, it cuts to the chase. And the heart.

Explore

- Telling myself that I matter makes me feel . . . (Notice any weather that arises and breathe into it.)
- Without apology and hesitation, I would like to declare . . .

DAY 203
CHECK IN—BEING BOLD, BEING VULNERABLE

Courage is derived from the word *coeur*, which means "heart" in French. The focus this week was to explore what it means to live a wholehearted life, to see how courage and vulnerability work together to complete you.

What helps you move through fear and embrace vulnerability? In what ways do you feel more courageous now? How do you know the truth when you hear it?

Explore

- What helps me move through fear and embrace vulnerability . . .
- Ways that I feel more courageous . . .
- How I know the truth when I hear it . . .

WEEK 30
ALLOWING IMPERFECTION

To Taoism that which is absolutely still or absolutely perfect is absolutely dead, for without the possibility for growth and change there can be no Tao. In reality there is nothing in the universe which is completely perfect or completely still; it is only in the minds of men that such concepts exist.

—Alan Watts

DAY 204
MOVING BEYOND FEAR

Back in the eighties, we had a next-door neighbor who was a preeminent emergency room doctor. During his off-hours Jerry would practice piano, study Russian, and direct plays in his tiny basement home theater (yes, complete with stage, sound, and lighting) for select audiences.

His example puts into sharp contrast the countless times I've resisted acting on a deeper yearning because of fear: fear of failing, getting it wrong, not being liked. Fear that I'll be rejected, ridiculed, or shamed. Fear that I'm taking up too much space, making too much noise, asking too much.

Or just the plain old *memory* of fear.

All that fear! God, it's exhausting and nauseating to see it laid out like that. I can feel my entire body and breathing contract.

Perfectionism is a tyranny of the worst kind.

Explore

- Some of the ways that I've allowed fear to stop me from doing something I really wanted (needed) . . .
- One fear that could use some "loving up" (acceptance and forgiveness) right now is . . .

DAY 205
IT'S NOT OVER

The important appointment you missed. The call you forgot to return. The email you sent that you wish you hadn't. The favorite sweater that shrunk beyond recognition . . . You know, those heart-stopping moments when you realize that you have royally screwed up.

Yes, we've all gulped and gasped and OMG-ed. We've all been in that gnawingly awful space of wanting to turn back the clock so bad and not being able to. We've all thrashed around in the messy, imperfect wreckage that we helped create, where it's all over and *too late!*

Or at least that's what it feels like when we're in a high state of alert. It may be too late to reverse a wrong, but it's never too late to reverse a crisis in our head: to quiet the mind and nourish the heart. It is never too late to admit the error of our ways, apologize, and cut ourselves some slack.

It may take some extra work, but there *is* something we can do when we've made a mistake. We can simply *be* with it.

What is one thing you wish you could reverse? Allow yourself to just be with that.

Explore

- One thing I wish I could reverse . . .
- What it feels like to just be with the memory of it . . . (Observe and allow all the squirminess, frustration, disappointment to arise for as long as you can handle it.)

DAY 206
MESS UP

Screwups or opportunities? When was the last time you made a mistake that you owned fair and square? When was the last time you (or someone else) made a mistake and you just let it be?

Mistakes go with the territory of clearing. They come in all shapes and sizes. The good news is that they offer us an opportunity to grow and evolve by showing us where, and how, we hold on.

In spacious-speak, the concept of wanting to get something right is simply the mind doing its efforting dance when it doesn't like something, or is attached to something, or is remembering something . . . *from the past.*

Next time you do something embarrassing or second-guess yourself, use it as an opportunity to do nothing about it for one minute.

Yes, nothing. No fixing, no changing, no improving, no managing. Just notice it simply as weather passing through you for you to observe. And allow.

What does screwing up feel like, and where in the body do you feel it exactly?

Explore

- What it feels like to sit with a mistake . . . (and where I feel it . . .)
- Watching a mistake play itself out while still owning it fully feels . . .

DAY 207
"BE WITH NOW" MEDITATION

How about now? Would now work? Can you accept and allow things to be just as they are in this very moment?

When it comes to present time, there is nothing special you need to be, or do, or make happen. Now is all there is. And you're living it. The real question to ask yourself is, can you live in it with full awareness?

If you have trouble being the zone of now, today's meditation will help. Reach for it especially when you're feeling impatient, anxious, frustrated, or overwhelmed, and follow these steps for at least one minute. They will help to quiet the mind and pull you back from the brink.

1. **Close your eyes,** and take a deep breath in and a slow, emptying breath out.
2. When you feel centered, slowly **breathe in** the phrase "I am here," and **breathe out** the phrase "I am now."
3. **Repeat** the sequence a few more times until you feel your breath slowing and your nervous system calming.
4. When you feel ready, **switch** to a second set of phrases: **Breathe in** the phrase "I accept," and **breathe out** the phrase "I allow."
5. Again, **repeat** a few more times, alternating between the two sets of phrases.

6. **Open your eyes** when you feel complete, and reflect in your journal on the following prompts.

Can you accept and allow things to be just as they are?

Explore
- It is safe for me to accept and allow things as they are because . . .
- The part of me that doesn't feel so safe . . .

DAY 208
SAY YES TO NOW

Take a minute today to consider this question by Brené Brown:

What would you be glad that you did, even if you failed?

Would it be okay to say yes to something even if you failed?

Explore
- What I would be glad I did even if I failed . . .
- What it feels like to say yes to something that might not work out . . .

DAY 209
HEART SPEAK

I love Maira Kalman's beautiful, stream-of-consciousness book, *My Favorite Things*. Here's an excerpt:

Naps under trees.
Blurry thoughts.
Breaths.
Angry thoughts.
Breaths.
Trees.

In just a few words, she takes us inside her heart. It reads like breathing itself.

Try it: Take one minute today to write down your own stream of consciousness "poem" that reflects what you are experiencing in the moment. Don't censor yourself. Just let the pen go and the heart speak.

What does being present feel like? What does it reveal?

Explore

- My one-minute now "poem" . . .
- What my one-minute now reveals . . .

DAY 210
CHECK IN—ALLOWING IMPERFECTION

The focus this week was to allow and experience imperfection as a fully formed, legitimate state of being, and to use it as a pathway to clearing some of the crusty stuff that holds you back from realizing a deeper yearning.

In what ways do you feel that you need to be in control? What does it feel like to enter into the quiet space of accepting and allowing things to be as they are? And what gets in your way? Do you notice any shifting of energy by simply giving your discomfort some witnessing space?

Explore

- Some of the ways I need to be in control . . . (and what that feels like . . .)
- Ways I can honor myself (especially after screwing up) . . .
- What I notice when I give my imperfection some space . . .

W E E K 3 1
WAITING IT OUT

You can't plan everything.
>—Lorne Michaels,
>executive producer of *Saturday Night Live*

DAY 211
MOMMY MONKEY MIND

How many times have you put your best foot forward and still come up exhausted and empty-handed? You know those days when all your carefully crafted plans suddenly go *poof!* and you're left standing there wondering what the heck happened and asking yourself, "What do I do next?"

A desperate email from my daughter, who had just missed her train connection while traveling abroad, reminded me of the times when world systems conspire against me despite my best intentions; times when I've pushed through tears and fears to keep from completely collapsing in a heap on the floor. This email from her brought it all home:

> I am exhausted from running through the stations with my luggage. Almost cried at the ticket window for no reason when I missed my train. I alternate between: It happens and I kind of want my parents. I know I am 20 and I can handle this. It happens, it really does, and I really do understand it. But I miss you. And after 4 train switches today, 4 different stations to navigate, and not sleeping at all in my hostels the past few nights, I feel the adventure but I also feel tired, and a little sad.

First world problems aside, if you're a parent or a surrogate parent, you'll know that an email like this doesn't always sit well. No matter how old the "kid" is.

Notice what goes through your mind the next time you get hijacked by fear. Can you enter into the experience without getting lost in it?

Explore

- When my best plans come up empty, I feel . . .
- One thing that can help me stay present in my discomfort is . . .

DAY 212
SHIFT HAPPENS

As I read about my only child sitting stranded in a melted heap in a foreign railway station, I watched my helpless "mommy monkey mind" jockeying for a spin down the familiar rabbit hole of anxiety and fear.

Out of somewhere came the strength to reply with what I knew deep in my bones was the real truth: that it was all going to work out somehow. I said a prayer and waited for something to change.

Less than five minutes after my daughter and I had spoken, up popped this email from her:

Found a hotel around the corner that is offering amazing last-minute discounts on their premium rooms. And I got one! All good.

Shift happens. Especially when you make room for it.

Explore

- If I wait a little longer for difficult situations to sort them-selves out, I notice . . .
- What it feels like to let things be . . .

DAY 213
WAIT IT OUT

Is there something you're noodling on, something that's unsettling you or keeping you up at night? If so, take a step back. Pause. Breathe. Give the situation some space to play itself out. Allow the nudgy feelings of frustration, overwhelm, or even despair to arise.

Sit with the discomfort, like you're sitting with a dear friend, until something shifts. See if letting things be for a bit doesn't resolve the situation or create an opening you didn't see coming.

Explore

- Something I'm noodling on is . . .
- When I wait and watch what happens, I notice . . .

DAY 214
GOING YOUR WAY

I love how we can input a street address into our cell phones and instantly see the various routes to our destination. Some are more direct and faster, others more scenic and slower. We get to choose.

If you think of life as a continuous, unfolding adventure leading you toward one destination—the realization of your purpose here on earth—it really doesn't matter which path you ultimately choose. You can't lose.

Next time you find yourself at a big crossroads—stressing about a career path, or a move that could radically change your life—give it some space. Don't exhaust yourself trying to figure out what has not yet been revealed.

Trust, and take heart. Divine intelligence is at work and has your back. All paths will take you where you want to go. Can you allow yourself to be led?

Explore

- I believe my purpose here on earth is to . . .
- Given a choice between a direct and indirect route to the realization of my dreams, I prefer to take . . .

DAY 215
THINGS ALWAYS WORK OUT

If you were to look back on your life, you might just notice that things have always worked out for you. Yes, even things like pain and loss have worked out to give you insight and perspective.

In hindsight, have you noticed if things work out better if you don't try so hard and let go of attachment to the outcome?

Take a look back and reflect in your journal how life has unfolded for you. Use this opportunity to discover what pathways tend to work best for you.

Explore

- One of the ways that things have worked out for me without my having to try so hard is . . .
- Things work out better for me when . . .

DAY 216
BEST ESCAPE

When the comedian Amy Poehler was asked to fill in the blank for "Best Escape" in an issue of *O, The Oprah Magazine*, her reply was:

> My closet. A lot of people forget that you can go hide in there next to your favorite sweater, close your eyes, and reset. All you need is ten minutes.

What helps you press the reset button in your life?

Explore
- My best escape . . .
- I know I am "reset" when . . .

DAY 217
CHECK IN—WAITING IT OUT

The focus this week was to notice what happens when you give things space to sort themselves out.

What does it feel like to take your time? What happens when you hang in there just a little longer in those "crisis" situations? Have you noticed a pattern to how your life has unfolded so far?

Explore
- When I take my time, I feel . . .
- It is safe for me to take my time because . . . (Notice the part of you that isn't quite sure.)
- It is safe for me to trust that things will work out because . . .

WEEK 32
SINGING PRAISES

You are a marvel.

—Pablo Casals

DAY 218
VALIDATION

There's an adorable video on YouTube that's been around for years called "Validation." It never fails to lift me up. I've watched it about fifteen times.

Professionally made, it is a parable on the power of positive reinforcement. It features a parking garage ticket validator whose mission is to cheer people up by telling them how awesome they are. Once he's filled up each person with his praises, he stamps their ticket with a big VALIDATED stamp. He becomes so popular that people stand in line for hours to see him.

How does what you say (or don't say) affect those around you? Try it with praise: Give someone a compliment today. You might want to stretch with this a little by choosing someone you don't know, don't like, or feel a bit squeamish around.

Notice how complimenting someone else makes *you* feel.

Explore
- When I compliment someone, I notice . . .
- Complimenting someone I don't know (or don't like) feels . . .
- Complimenting others makes me feel . . .

DAY 219
YOUR UNIVERSE TALKING

Here's a message from your universe by the highly acclaimed cellist, Pablo Casals, in his book *Joys and Sorrows*:

> Do you know what you are? You are a marvel. You are unique. . . . In all the years that have passed, there has never been another child like you. Your legs, your arms, your clever fingers, the way you move.

> You may become a Shakespeare, a Michaelangelo [*sic*], a Beethoven. You have the capacity for anything.

> Yes, he's talking about YOU. Take it in.

Explore
- The last time I received a compliment from someone was . . .
- It was easy (or hard) for me to receive it because . . .

DAY 220
PRAISES LIGHTEN

I can't think of a single person who doesn't light up even just a teeny bit after being praised. We humans need genuine acknowledgment, right up there with water and air.

So why is it so hard for some of us to take in praise or recognition when it is freely offered? Or give it?

Explore

- When someone compliments me, I feel . . .
- It is easier (or harder) to give a compliment than to receive one because . . .

DAY 221
50 AMAZING THINGS

Today is a big day! We're going to take a tip from Dr. Wayne Dyer and do an exercise from his book *I Am* that'll fill up your tank really fast. Consider this quote:

> Any time you start a sentence with *I am,* you are creating what you are and what you want to be.

Now, take out your journal and download fifty amazing things about yourself beginning with the words "I am . . ."

Don't think about it too much, and don't be bashful. Go for the gusto, lay it on thick, and notice any stuck energy that is moved by naming and writing it down. (Bookmark this page in your journal and return to it anytime you're feeling down, out of sorts, or under the weather. It will help you come back to your center.)

Explore

- It was easy (or hard) to come up with fifty positive qualities about myself because . . .
- The bottom-line most amazing thing about myself is . . . (Write this one on a sticky note and place it in a location where you'll see it every day.)

DAY 222
CURSE OR BENEFIT?

Using a four-letter word reduces the stress response. True or false?

I can see how cursing as a way to vent can be a useful tool. I certainly have been known to reach for a few choice expletives to release pent-up frustration and emotional charge before.

Cursing can also injure if it is used as a weapon to hurt another, or to avoid taking responsibility. As a low-vibrational frequency, it can backfire and create more stress in the environment if it isn't used consciously.

Not about good or bad. In my view, it boils down to energetics. Four-letter words carry an energetic charge. Used in a safe, contained way, they come in handy sometimes to off-gas and release charge.

Explore
- Cursing works (or doesn't work) for me because . . .
- Curse words that help me vent . . . (and what it feels like to write them down . . .)

DAY 223
YOU ARE LOVEABLE

How are you loveable? How do you know you are loveable?

In his book *Loveability,* Robert Holden says, "The goal of this journey is not to find love; it is to know love. This knowledge exists in you already. I call this knowledge *loveability*."

Does this subject bring up any queasiness? Can you allow squeamish resistance to surface without giving it any energy? The path to self-love may be riddled with bumps, potholes, and detours, but no one can walk it for you. If you're willing to put one baby step in front of another, and feel your way through to the sweet, loveable self that you are, it will be the most rewarding journey you will ever take.

Explore
- I am loveable because . . .
- When I repeat the phrase "I am lovable," I feel . . .

DAY 224
CHECK IN—SINGING PRAISES

This week we studied the power of validation and the energetic impact that positive and negative words can have on us.

How does what you say affect those around you? Can you feel the energy change (in the other person, yourself, the space) when you compliment someone versus when you critique them?

What did it feel like to make a list of fifty positive things about yourself? Did you feel you could keep going, or did you feel like you had to fake it to come up with the full fifty?

If you didn't do the exercise, take a moment today to consider why, and ask yourself why you're not making time for yourself. (If that invitation just pressed a button, congratulations. You get to clear more squirmy stuff by hanging out with it.)

Explore
- Words that lift my spirits and lighten my load . . .
- Doing the Fifty Amazing Things About Me exercise revealed . . .
- I'm not doing the exercise(s) because . . . (Notice any twinges of guilt, resistance, or shame, and breathe into them.)

WEEK 33
CULTIVATING SELF-CARE

I was going to work-out, but then realized . . . this nap isn't going to take itself.

—someecards.com

DAY 225
SAY YES TO NO

I love the Anne Taintor card of a woman lounging in bed in her silk nightgown and satin sheets, looking upward at nothing in particular, contemplating her exquisite and uncomplicated life. The caption reads, "I love not camping."

Fifties glamour and electric blanket aside, this card says it all on so many levels. How often do we feel remorseless about taking time to do something just for ourselves? Or have the clarity to know what we don't really want? Or have the courage to opt out of doing something that feels like a "should" and might disappoint someone?

What is one thing you can say no to today that doesn't serve or support you? And what can you do instead that feels super good?

Explore
- One thing I can say no to . . .
- One thing that I can opt for that feels super good . . .

DAY 226
SAY YES TO SELF-CARE

What is one act of self-care that nudges you out of your comfort zone?

Perhaps it's taking a nap in the middle of the day. Or watching one of your guilty pleasures on TV without having to apologize for it. Maybe it's letting a family member sort out a problem on his or her own.

Whatever it is, say yes today to self-care, and no to anything that does not serve and support you.

And allow the squirmy monkey mind to not like it one bit.

Explore
- It's easy (or not easy) for me to satisfy a guilty pleasure because . . .
- What I can say yes to today (without apology) . . .

DAY 227
SELF-CARE IS THE BALM

Self-care is not an extracurricular activity. It is not something we do when we're sick or everyone else in the house or workplace is taken care of. It is a necessity. Like food and breathing.

Self-care goes hand in glove with clearing. Every time you step out of your comfort zone to clear things and thoughts, you are bringing in more light, moving more energy, *and* triggering the stress response.

Self-care is the balm. It works to calm down the nervous system, help you feel safe, and bring you back into balance.

PS The "self" part of self-care means precisely that: by yourself, for yourself—*not* for your spouse, mother, child, dog, neighbor, or best friend! We cannot possibly be of service to anyone when we are overextended and our circuits are fried.

Explore

- The thought of applying self-care like a balm to anything that ails me makes me feel . . .

- It feels good (or not good) to choose myself over the needs of others because . . .

DAY 228
WHY SELF-CARE WORKS

The self-care model works because it moves beyond the mind's capacity to rationalize and into the part of us that *knows:* the heart.

The monkey mind, with its endless litany of well-crafted comebacks, is unhinged in the presence of pure ease: *It's not that simple; If you knew what my life was like; I've tried slowing down, taking baths, lighting candles, but they don't last; I'm back to being stressed again . . .* the list goes on. When you're going up against all this noise, it's important to stop, take a deep breath, and remember that this is a stressed-out mind talking, not the real you.

What do you do to sabotage your ease? What can you do right now to shift it?

Explore

- Some of the stories I tell myself that sabotage my self-care . . .

- Reframing these excuses and doubts feels . . .

DAY 229
CREATE CLEAR BOUNDARIES

There's a funny cartoon of a woman sunbathing on the beach. She's a complete blob of exhaustion, soaking up a much-needed vacation. Her husband is handing her the cell phone, saying, "It's the hospital. They want to know if it would be too much trouble to fly back to work a shift."

Managing a request while you're miles away on vacation may be a no-brainer. But what about the countless times you're just about to sit down for a quiet moment over dinner and the phone rings? Or your boss has you stay longer because this assignment "just cannot wait"? Or your email inbox is invaded by messages you never subscribed to?

I would wager that your boundaries have been crossed hundreds of times. And here's the tough-love truth that may be a bit harder to hear: You've allowed it to happen.

Take a few minutes today to reflect on what it would take to set clear boundaries, and what gets in your way.

Explore
- My boundaries that have been crossed . . .
- What I need to do to set a clearer boundary . . .

DAY 230
WAYS TO OPT OUT GRACEFULLY

For some of us who have been brought up to be polite and not rock the boat, saying no can feel like a dagger to the heart. We would rather contort ourselves into pretzels of unease than speak our truth.

If it's hard for you to say no and set clear boundaries with others, consider these gentle approaches to grow your self-care muscle:

- **Decline graciously** with, "Thanks for asking. I'm sorry it's not going to work for me this time."
- **Turn it over to voicemail:** Put a message on your voicemail letting callers know that it may take a few days for you to return their call.
- **Add an away message:** Put an auto-reply message on your email saying that you will be out and will not be responding to any emails until a certain date.
- **Unsubscribe** from email lists that no longer serve and support you; cancel your subscription to a newspaper or magazine that you never read.

Opting out doesn't have to be onerous. Put yourself first and keep it simple: no fuss, no charge, no guilt. And if you do feel twinges of missing out, guilt, or remorse, use it as an opportunity to clear (embrace) the discomfort with compassionate awareness.

(Remember, it goes both ways: If you're attached to being in control or needed by others, that is another issue that needs addressing as well.)

Explore
- The situations that are the hardest for me to opt out of are . . . (because . . .)
- One thing I would like to opt out of today is . . .

DAY 231
CHECK IN—CULTIVATING SELF-CARE

The focus this week was on cultivating nourishing self-care. Given how we've been raised, it's no surprise to see how wired we are to serve others at the expense of ourselves.

What would a should-free life feel like? What can you do to set clear boundaries and care deeply for yourself?

Explore

- It is safe for me to let go of the shoulds and cultivate self-care because . . .
- An affirmation or mantra I can adopt to remind me to honor and care for myself is . . . (It could be "I choose ease," "It's safe for me to say no," or "Caring for myself lifts others," for example.)

WEEK 34
NOURISHING
SELF-WORTH

If you show up for yourself in your life, the universe will show up for you.

—Madisyn Taylor, "Actively Participating," *DailyOM*

DAY 232
CHOOSE YOURSELF

"Me, me! Pick me!"

I love watching children raise their hands as high as they can to be called on by their teacher. I love when they scream, "Look at me, mommy! Look at me!" (Read: "Look how great I am!")

Where did our beautiful self-selecting exuberance go? Where did our unapologetic joy disappear to? Why is it so hard to stand up and advocate for ourselves as adults?

It's a sad day when we retreat into our safe houses of politeness and surrender to what the collective has dictated is best. The paradigm that has made us feel bad for shining our light too brightly serves no one.

In what ways are you still putting yourself last? What are you doing to change the paradigm of self-neglect? What can you do today to advocate for yourself?

Explore

- I choose myself now because . . .
- What gets in the way of this is . . .
- One thing I can do today to advocate for myself is . . .

DAY 233
SELF-LESS VERSUS SELF-MORE

Honoring your feelings without apology. Being willing to disappoint and be disappointed. Having it be okay to fail. Giving yourself massive amounts of slack when you screw up. Setting clear boundaries. Advocating for your soul.

This is what it means to choose yourself.

When you hold a space for yourself in this way, you make yourself more available, compassionate, and spacious with others.

It's a win-win.

Explore

- It is safe for me to put myself first because . . . (Notice the part that doesn't feel so comfortable.)
- One way I can hold a space for myself today . . .

DAY 234
HONOR YOURSELF NO MATTER WHAT

Yes, I know. We forget. With a monkey mind piping in at all hours, the last thing we remember to do is honor ourselves no matter what.

Embracing the good, the bad, and the ugly sides of ourselves—*all* of it—is not for the faint of heart. Growing ourselves is messy business, and there is no one who illustrates it better than Anne Lamott. She nails it in this piece she wrote for *O, The Oprah Magazine* called "Becoming the Person You Were Meant to Be: Where to Start":

> Here's how I became myself: mess, failure, mistakes, disappointments, and extensive reading; limbo, indecision, setbacks, addiction, public embarrassment, and endless conversations with my best women friends; the loss of people without whom I could not live, the loss of pets that left me reeling, dizzying betrayals but much greater loyalty, and overall, choosing as my motto William Blake's line that we are here to learn to endure the beams of love.

It is not a perfect science, but if you add heaps of love and self-care to your life every day, it is going to change.

And so will you.

Explore

- One way that my life is already changing . . .
- One way I can honor myself today . . .

DAY 235
DISAPPOINT

Today's practice might rattle your cage a bit, especially if you're attached to what people think of you.

Here's the invitation: Do or say something today that might disappoint somebody, be misconstrued, or be hard for others to hear. You do not need to reveal a deep, dark secret about yourself; this exercise is simply an opportunity to stretch a bit more into supporting the truth of who you are.

Okay, ready?

B-r-e-a-t-h-e.

The breath is always a good place to start.

Honestly, if you really think about it, disappointing someone is not the hard part. We unintentionally do it all the time. The harder part is doing it full on—with awareness.

Explore

- Disappointing someone feels . . .
- It is safe for me to say or do something that might disappoint because . . .

DAY 236
HOW ARE YOU?

We've all done it. We've all mumbled the generic "fine" when asked how we're doing. There's never any life in it.

What would happen if we told the truth, as Maya Angelou suggests in her book *Letter to My Daughter*?

Let's tell the truth to people. When people ask, "How are you" have the nerve sometimes to answer truthfully. You must know however, that people will start avoiding you because they too have knees that pain them and heads which hurt and they don't want to know about yours. But think of it this way: if people avoid you, you will have more time to meditate and do fine research on a cure for whatever truly afflicts you.

Next time someone asks you how you're doing, what will you say?

Explore

- *How am I doing?* I'm doing . . .
- The idea of sharing exactly how I feel is easy (or not easy) for me because . . .

DAY 237
FEED YOUR SOUL

Realizing our deepest yearnings is soul work, and the slow-drip clearing we've been practicing is so that we can uncover and nourish those yearnings.

In her book *Gift from the Sea,* Anne Morrow Lindbergh writes,

> The problem is not entirely in finding the room of one's own, the time alone, difficult and necessary as this is. The problem is more how to still the soul in the midst of its activities. In fact, the problem is how to feed the soul.

How are you feeding your soul?

It's a wonder question—not something you need to answer, but instead sit with, contemplate, and live.

Explore

- My soul needs . . .
- Ways that I feed my soul . . .
- One thing I can do today to feed my soul is . . .

DAY 238
CHECK IN—NOURISHING SELF-WORTH

The focus over the past few weeks has been to fill up our tanks by validating, honoring, and supporting ourselves with care. Each small step we take to advocate for ourselves changes the paradigm from self-neglect to self-nourishment.

In what ways do you recognize that putting yourself first makes you more available to others? That holding a space for yourself creates a space for others? That feeding your soul feeds others?

It may not always be easy, welcomed, or well received, but when we raise our energy level, we effectively raise the energy of others.

Explore
- When I raise my energy level, I notice . . .
- Some of the changes I'm noticing as a result of my daily practices in self-nourishment are . . .
- Right now I am feeling . . .

WEEK 35
STEPPING INTO STILLNESS

We can make our minds so like still water that beings gather about us that they may see, it may be, their own images, and so live for a moment with a clearer, perhaps even with a fiercer life because of our quiet.

—William Butler Yeats,
"Earth, Fire and Water," *The Celtic Twilight*

DAY 239
REAL QUIET

When was the last time you experienced a day of quiet so deep and restorative that it felt like you were floating? Or breathing in pure oxygen?

Quiet—as in the absence of noise—should be put on the world's most endangered species list. Our world has become so noisy that we've forgotten what Real Quiet feels like.

I can't remember a time I ever felt so deeply nourished by silence until we landed in a remote part of Italy—miles away from the nearest town—to celebrate the wedding of our nephew. As soon as I got out of the car, I could feel my entire being expand, fluff out like a pillow that had been crammed and sealed in one of those plastic storage bags for too long.

No distant traffic sounds, no police sirens, no blaring horns, no lawn mowers, no leaf blowers, no manhole covers thwacking with each passing car, no refrigerators whirring in the next room, no WiFi, no cell service . . .

What greeted us for three whole days was pure, delicious silence—with a touch of birdsong, rustling wind through trees, and a random cowbell.

It was heaven.

Imagine what it would feel like if everyone on the planet did one small thing every day to turn down the noise. (Even just turning down a TV set that no one is watching would be a step in the right direction.)

I daresay we might be breathing more deeply, if not smiling more.

Explore

- When things are quiet, I feel . . .
- What my life would be like if it were quiet . . .
- One thing I can do to bring more quiet to my life . . .

DAY 240
SLOW DOWN

I've carried around in my head and heart a phrase that's proved beneficial over and over again: "When you are rushed, vital connections are lost." Marianne Williamson agrees, and wrote on Facebook the following:

> Every big mistake I've made in my life was made because I was moving too fast. If Spirit whispers anything, it's "Slow down, slow down, slow down, slow down." A flash of lightening can bring inspiration, but only depth of reflection brings wisdom.

What happens to you when you move too fast?

Explore

- When I move too fast, I notice . . .
- It is safe for me to slow down because . . . (Name and feel any part of you that doesn't feel so safe.)

DAY 241
THE RENEWING MAGIC OF GRACE

Back in the days when I was first learning to clear spaces, I would get sick a lot. The "clearing" would show up mostly in the form of garden-variety head colds. This piece I wrote years ago reflects a turning point in how I related to the experience:

A tickle in my throat has turned into a full-blown, unrelenting hack-a-thon. I've spent days waking up in a trash heap of sweat, cough drop wrappers, and remedies.

Mystified that this storm system, which has settled like a squatter in my throat and chest, appears to be going nowhere fast. No change, no progress, no light at the end of this particular tunnel. Not pretty.

I can feel the mind sitting there, just salivating to go on a field day of worst-case scenarios.

If I let it.

This morning appeared to be no different from all the others, except for one (significant) thing: I detached.

I took a sip of water, laid myself back down on the heaping chaos that is my bed, and decided not to fight anymore. In an instant, there it was.

Stillness.

The enveloping, quieting, renewing magic . . . of grace.

Have you ever had an experience of deep stillness? Where were you? What did it feel like? How could you cultivate more of it?

Explore
- What stillness feels like for me . . .
- One way I can cultivate more of it . . .

DAY 242
FLIP THE SWITCH

The word "labor" sounds so . . . painful. And exhausting. Yet, we spend most of our days unconsciously laboring. Laboring at the computer; laboring over what to wear; laboring over what to cook for dinner; laboring over to-do lists that never seem to get done; laboring over what people think; laboring over the state of our homes, our kids, our weight, our finances, our hair . . .

All the while, Labor's sibling, Stillness, waits and watches in what I can only imagine is amused silence.

What if choosing stillness over labor could be as simple as flipping a switch inside you? What if it could be an experience that you could simply call in, or step into, or rest inside of?

Try it today: Close your eyes and imagine an invisible light switch inside your heart space. Flip it on and invite stillness to fill, lift, and illuminate you. Notice what happens to your sense of ease, peace, and wonder.

Explore

- Inviting stillness to fill me up feels . . .
- If stillness could speak, it would tell me . . .

DAY 243
TEN WAYS TO CULTIVATE STILLNESS— ONE MINUTE AT A TIME

With a monkey mind in constant motion, it's easy to forget how to ease into stillness. So I put together a list of ten practices—culled from this book—that will help you quiet the noise and feel good.

1. **Rest in beauty:** Look up from your screen and place your attention on something beautiful. Allow your mind to rest in that.

2. **Take your time:** Deliberately slow down for one minute when your impulse is to speed up (and allow yourself to squirm).

3. **Insert awareness:** Release tension by observing it. See if tightness eases by being a witnessing presence.

4. **Be curious:** Pretend you know nothing; invite wonder; accept mystery as a legitimate state of being.

5. **Wait and watch:** Allow an answer to reveal itself through one of your senses. Don't force or overthink it.

6. **Do nothing:** Allow things to be just as they are without doing anything to fix or change them.

7. **Don't personalize:** Pretend that everything that does not feel good is not yours. Repeat, "It's not mine."

8. **Breathe and release:** Breathe deeply from your chest, down to your belly, through the soles of your feet, and into the earth.

9. **Wash and release**: Use the simple practice of washing your hands (body, dishes) for one minute to quiet your mind and release stress.

10. **Sit in silence:** Sit quietly for one minute with no agenda.

What are some of your favorite ways to slow down and be still?

Explore

- Ways that work for me to cultivate quiet stillness . . .
- What it feels like to simply read the list . . .

DAY 244
MAGIC IN REPETITION—
A TEN-DAY PRACTICE

One of the keys to success in clearing, as you know, is repetition. In my world, repetition means daily. No matter what your clearing challenge is, or how little time you have to devote to it, it will get easier if you make it part of a daily routine. Using the list of one-minute practices from yesterday's message you can try it for ten days and see what happens. These simple guidelines will help:

1. **Start** at the top of the list and go down the list for ten days. Alternatively, choose the same approach and repeat it each day for ten days. Choose the same time of day if possible.

2. At the end of each session, **close your eyes**. Take a deep breath and notice how you feel.

3. **Notice** your breathing before and after the practice.
4. Add a **reminder note** to your calendar to check in with yourself at the end of ten days. Notice what happens to your overall sense of ease and well-being at the end of that time.

(PS You don't need to stop at ten days. Keep cycling through these until they become easy and effortless.)

Explore
- After one minute of cultivating stillness, I feel . . .
- After ten days, I feel . . .

DAY 245
CHECK IN—STEPPING INTO STILLNESS

While continuing on the larger theme of self-care, the focus this week was to cultivate quiet stillness and deep rest.

How easy (or hard) is it to step into and rest in stillness? Are you finding that your one minute is growing into more minutes? If not, perhaps the mind is still not ready to dial it down as much as you'd like. Try again with one practice that does not elicit a resisting response.

What is one practice you can truly integrate into your life for a week or ten days that would feel really good? This is the place to start.

Explore
- It is easy (or hard) to cultivate quiet stillness in my life because . . .
- It is safe for me to quiet the mind because . . .
- I can make more time to rest if I . . .

WEEK 36
HOMING IN ON JOY

Isn't that the only way to curate a life? To live among things that
make you gasp with delight?
—Maira Kalman, *My Favorite Things*

DAY 246
A HAPPY HOME

Sleeping in . . . on a supremely cushy bed, with soft sheets and the
perfect pillow. Sipping a fabulous cup of coffee in a sunny window seat
from a mug that I cradle with both hands. Taking time to do something
for myself. Saying no and not feeling guilty afterward. Taking a hot bath
with sea salt and baking soda.

These are some of the things that make me feel complete, unadulterated joy.

As we prepare this week to explore how our state of being affects the
spaces that we occupy, use today to reflect on the truth of this statement:
"There is no mistaking the delicious spaciousness of a happy home."

Explore
- When I walk into a happy home, I feel . . .
- What brings me pure, unadulterated joy . . .
- One thing I can do today to cultivate joy is . . .

DAY 247
HAPPILY GROOVING

It seems that my happily grooving at home might be contagious. According to a *Boston Globe* article by Carolyn Johnson, it has been scientifically proven that happiness ripples beyond your inner circle of friends:

> It seems obvious that your closest friends might influence your mood, but the study found that even the happiness of a friend's friend boosts your chance of being happy by 9.8 percent. Even more surprising, the happiness of a friend of a friend of a friend boosts your chance of being happy by 5.6 percent.

This study, published in the prominent *British Medical Journal,* also said that the effects can last a year!

So if you suddenly wake up feeling inexplicably joyous, it could be just plain you, or something beaming at you from the air or the water. Your neighbor's neighbor's happiness just might wind and waft its way over to you and catch you off guard, lift you up, and slap a smile on your face for no apparent reason. And if you're one of those eternally optimistic, upbeat, happy-go-lucky types, it's possible that you're doing more good for the planet than you even know.

Explore
- The last time I felt really happy was . . .
- One thing I could do today to experience more of it . . .

DAY 248
CONDUCT YOUR OWN HAPPINESS STUDY

I'm not sure we really need a study to prove there is an invisible connective tissue of thoughts and feelings that binds us humans to each other. If you're awake and aware in your body and open in your heart, you will *know*.

You don't have to take my word for it. Conduct your own study in the weeks and months to come. Notice if your sense of ease, peace, or joy has any effect on your home, family, a neighbor, colleague, friend, or even a loved one living on the other side of world! If you're not feeling at ease, peaceful, or joyful just yet, you can always try faking it 'til you make it. This underrated tip is always helpful in nudging you in the direction you want to go.

Notice how your state of being affects the world around you, and how the world, in turn, mirrors you back to you.

Explore
- Ways that I've noticed my world "out there" is mirroring me back to me . . .
- One simple step I can take that raises the vibration of happiness in my home . . .

DAY 249
SPACE SHIFTING

If you were to join me on a space clearing consultation of someone's home or workplace, you might notice how some areas feel clear and others more congested (yes, even in spaces that have no visible clutter).

By tuning in with your six senses (smell, taste, touch, hearing, sight, and intuition), you would be able to follow the energy streams that snake through a living space. You might perceive all kinds of energy signatures, from negative thought patterns and emotional charge on one end of the spectrum to the sparkly frequencies of love, spaciousness, and joy. You might notice that these palpable energies mirror our emotional state and can expand and contract on a dime.

Play with this concept for a few days in a row, if you can, and see if by changing the energy in yourself you notice a palpable shift in energy in your space:

1. **Choose a room** that feels cluttered, congested, or contracted.

2. Take a deep breath in and out and **become fully present and aware:** Observe your judgments, your discomforts, your impulses to bolt or recoil. Notice and allow sounds, smells, sights, tastes, feelings, and intuitions with *no attachment* (this is key) to any particular outcome.

3. After you've had a chance to witness, **do something that feels good** and raises your energy level: Play your favorite music, dance, tidy up, beautify with flowers, meditate.

What shifts do you notice—in energy, ambient light, mood of fam ily members or pets—when you simply witness without attachment? Do you notice that by raising your vibration, you raise the energetic vibration of your space?

Explore

- Shifts that I notice in my space by simply being aware and not attached . . .
- I know that raising my energy level raises the energy of my space because . . .
- Changes that I've noticed in my space (and myself) over the past few days . . .

DAY 250
FEELING HOME

We've explored already how homes do not all feel the same, and how different spaces within the home can vary greatly from one another. It is easier to detect a sparkling living space when we compare it directly to one that is not so bright. The steps that follow will deepen your ability to tell the energetic difference between two spaces.

1. **Spend a few minutes in a space that feels cluttered**, unloved, untended, dark, congested. Notice your breathing, mood, and energy level.

2. **Repeat the exercise in a space that feels harmonious**, tended, light-filled, sparkly, and clutter-free. Go outdoors if you have to. Notice your breathing, mood, energy level.

3. **Be mindful** of your sensate and energy body. How do you feel during and after?

4. **Compare the two experiences.** How does each space feel physically? Mentally? Emotionally? Is it possible to compare the two without judging either as good or bad?

Explore

- What I experienced from tuning in to the energies of different living spaces . . .
- One small thing I can do today to change the way my home feels is . . .

DAY 251
THE JOY IN THINGS

Cultivating joy may not be as farfetched as it seems. The key, Geri Larkin tells us, is in starting small:

> The happiest person I have ever known was an elderly monk living up in the mountains of Korea. Everything he owned was in his room: robes, a tea set, a futon, a hat, tea, his sandals. Not only was he deliriously happy, giving off waves of giddy energy, but his room was incredibly beautiful in its simplicity. He allowed sunlight, and moonlight, to act as artists' brushes, emphasizing one corner now, the tea set later, the sandals another time.
>
> We can do this letting go. We can start small . . . The trick is to simply start.

What is one thing you love that you can pull out of hiding? What is one thing that you can display in your home that would bring you (delirious) joy?

Explore

- One thing I love that I can dust off and relocate to a place of honor . . .
- What it feels like to shine light on possessions that bring me joy . . .

DAY 252
CHECK IN—HOMING IN ON JOY

The focus this week was to home in on joy as a powerful energy signature that ripples out to affect everything and everyone around us; and to explore how raising our personal vibration changes how our spaces feel.

In what ways did you experience a direct connection between your state of being and the spaces you inhabit? What were some of the differences that you noticed when you compared a space that feels unloved and untended with one that is harmonious and "loved-up"? How did lifting a thing out of hiding elevate and (en)lighten you?

Explore
- Raising my personal energy level raises . . .
- Lightening up has enlightened me in the following surprising ways . . .

WEEK 37
FEELING GOOD

Whenever you are sincerely pleased, you are nourished.
—Ralph Waldo Emerson, "Considerations By the Way"

DAY 253
THE BEST BEAUTY TREATMENT

Have you ever stopped to wonder why some elders look so much younger than their peers? You could say it's genetics, geography, diet, having a sense of purpose or love in their life. No doubt all of these factors contribute to longevity and vitality.

If you ask me, I think it largely boils down to one thing: vibration. People who vibrate at the level of joy look and feel younger.

Joy is the champagne bubbles of living clear. It is the best beauty treatment I know of.

How does it feel to steep yourself in joy? You can find out by making an uncensored list of all the things, people, places, and experiences that bring (or have brought) you joy.

Explore
- What it feels like to steep in joy . . .
- My list of things, people, places, and experiences that I love . . .

DAY 254
NESTLE INTO COZY

It's nearly winter where I am as I write this, and I can't believe it's already pitch-dark outside. It's not even 5:00 p.m.!

Truth be told, there's a part of me that loves this time of year. Longer nights means more nesting time. Tea and blankie time. Cave time.

What I don't love is the mad rushing of the holiday season. It just doesn't match my internal need for more quiet and deep rest.

If you are feeling similarly misaligned and out of sorts (at *any* time of year), you might want to consider adopting some of my favorite ways to nestle into some delicious coziness:

- String some twinkly lights in your favorite room, and enjoy the space with all other lights turned off.
- Make a fabulous cup of coffee, tea, or hot chocolate and sip it by candlelight.
- Wrap yourself in a warm, fuzzy blankie.
- Take a nap or a catnap.
- Eat dinner in your twinkly room, or in bed.

What makes you feel supremely good? Make a list of five to ten things that help you dial down and feel safe and cozy.

Explore
- What makes me feel safe and cozy . . .
- Ways to dial it down . . .

DAY 255
BE DISCERNING

Truth time. On a scale of 1 to 10—with 10 being a joyful person who raises your energy level, cares about you, and would be there for you if you asked, and 1 being someone who is cheerless, self-involved, pessimistic, gossipy, and unsupportive of you—how would you describe the people you tend to hang out with?

If your circle is hovering below 7, maybe it's time to switch it up. Yes, like giving yourself an upgrade to first class.

Be with people who get you, who are more of a vibrational match to who you are becoming (or wish to become). In the end, you get to choose.

Explore
- People who love me, get me, and would be there for me if I asked . . .
- People who do not serve and support me any longer . . . (Remember, this is about vibration, not guilt or blame.)
- One thing I can do to switch up my relationships in a way that honors all concerned . . .

DAY 256
LIGHTEN UP

We all have those moments when we lose ourselves. You know, those times when we get consumed by self-importance and forget that we're on the planet to experience our birthright: joy.

What would happen if you declared today a "serious-free" day? A day where you take nothing seriously, and nothing personally. Oh heck, throw in "should-free" too, while you're at it.

Try it even just for an hour, and even if it messes with your mind, watch the energies shift.

Explore
- What happens when I take nothing seriously . . .
- What happens when I take nothing personally . . .
- Something I have taken way too seriously that I'm now ready to release . . .

DAY 257
SALT AND SODA REFRESH

I shared an all-purpose remedy in my first book, *Your Spacious Self*, that is worth mentioning again here because it is so simple and works like magic to smooth out the jangliness of a stressful day. It helps you feel better and sleep better too.

This simple formula was adapted from an old Edgar Cayce remedy by my friend, Bay Area teacher and healer Desda Zuckerman. Here's how it works:

- **Mix equal parts coarse sea salt** (or kosher salt) with household **baking soda**. (Desda recommends you use pure, coarse sea salt instead of Epsom salt.)
- **For a shower**, make a paste in your palm and rub it all over your body, including your hair, and shower off.
- **For a bath**, pour the mixture into the tub and soak.

Salt and soda mixed together as part of your shower or bath routine is an energy worker's best friend: it calms and eases any potential side-effects associated with clearing, restores balance, and integrates deep clearing.

Explore

- Some of the more subtle effects (on my body, mind, and spirit) of bathing in sea salt and baking soda are . . .
- What I notice about bathing before going to bed at night . . .
- Other ways that work to refresh me . . .

DAY 258
FEEL BETTER FAST

Today, I'm going to give you some quick practices that are designed to help lift, lighten, *and* enlighten. It's all about feeling good (or better) fast!

- **Round up** a space: Gather empty cups and plates, slide chairs back into place, power down devices, turn out unnecessary lights.
- **Shake out** the area rug in the kitchen, sweep the debris below it, and replace it.
- **Cook** something fragrant that wafts and lingers through the house.
- **Hang clothes** out to dry and enjoy the fresh, crisp smell when you take them down.
- **Light** a stick of Nag Champa incense.
- **Spritz** the air with a mixture of good water and a few drops of rose or lavender essential oil.
- **Do nothing at all,** with total awareness, for one minute.

How about you? What helps you to feel better fast?

Explore

- My list of top ways to feel better fast are . . .
- One thing I can do right now to feel better is . . .

DAY 259
CHECK IN—FEELING GOOD

The focus this week was to raise the vibration of joy—both internally and externally—by doing things that feel good.

In what ways have you noticed that you look and feel younger this week? Have you noticed a spring in your step? Or that your eyes and skin are brighter? What are some of your indicators that "steeping in joy" is working its magic?

Explore

- I know that steeping in joy is working its magic because . . .
- Some of the changes that I've noticed in my face and my body since I began my clearing journey . . .

WEEK 38
HONORING THE PAST

Gratitude makes sense of our past, brings peace for today, and creates a vision for tomorrow.
—Melody Beattie, *The Language of Letting Go*

DAY 260
"HEELING" THE PAST

My wedding shoes. I wore them just once on my wedding day twenty-nine years ago and I've kept them neatly in a box ever since.

Why?

Because these grass-stained relics remind me of the joyful day that I walked across a grassy knoll on the coast of Maine to marry my sweetheart and best friend. (Never mind that they take up space and no longer fit.)

The bigger question to ask of course is this: Is it possible to remember that magical day without carting around a box of shoes that I never open and will never wear from house to house, closet to closet? Is it possible to pull the box out and use it to practice letting go with compassionate awareness?

The short answer, of course, is yes.

The longer answer is that sometimes it takes as long as it takes to let things go.

No amount of coaxing or analyzing is going to move something out that door if the mind is spinning a memory from the past, feels duty-bound to save "just in case," or is caught in fight-or-flight survival mode.

The only way to unhinge a mind that is in lockdown is to clear things that *are* doable and won't activate the stress response.

After nearly three decades, I finally let the wedding shoes go. I took a photo of them and added the box to the mountain of stuff we took to Goodwill.

It was way easier than I expected, even if the grass stains in the photo do still elicit a smallish pang.

Explore

- One sentimental object I can pull out of hiding and begin the process of saying goodbye to is . . .
- Feelings that come up when I consider letting it go . . . (Remember that naming and feeling the emotional weather that arises—with compassionate awareness—is the real work here. It is not about "getting rid of" the object.)

DAY 261
RE-MEMBER

The word "remember" has a great deal of meaning. At its essence, it means to call back all of our "members"—those aspects in ourselves that we've neglected or have scattered or gone missing—and return to the truth of who we are.

And there is no better way to *pull yourself together*, I believe, than to adopt a simple daily practice in mindfulness and letting go.

What are you ready to let go of today?

Explore

- Something I've been keeping around "just in case" that no longer serves me or adds value . . .
- It is safe for me to honor it and let it go because . . . (Notice the part of you that wants to cling even more.)

DAY 262
ALTARS ARE EVERYWHERE

Though we mostly associate altars with churches or temples, they can be found everywhere. The special flower centerpiece on a Thanksgiving table and the good china place settings are a kind of altar. The photos on the refrigerator, the grouping of rocks and shells from a favorite beach or summer experience, the portrait holding court over the mantel, and the wreaths we hang to celebrate the seasons are just some of the ways we remember and connect with something timeless, something larger than ourselves.

Take a look around you today and notice some of the altars you've created in your home. Are there any that could use a little clearing or freshening up?

Explore

- Some of the altars that I've created to honor my past or a loved one . . .
- One altar that I love that could use some clearing or freshening up . . .

DAY 263
ALTARS ALTER

Altars offer a direct connection to spirit and a vehicle to experience spaciousness. You can use them to anchor an intention, quiet the mind, express gratitude, connect to your soul's deepest yearnings, honor the memory of a loved one, bless and release something or someone that no longer serves and supports you, or embrace, illuminate, call back . . . re-member.

Use today to place a small table or shelf in a quiet area of your home where you can imagine spending a minute or two every day. Once you've established your sacred spot, gather meaningful objects that symbolize a thing, person, habit, belief, painful memory, or outcome that you wish to release in your life. This could be an item of clothing, letters, food, a photo of your ex, words on a piece of paper . . . anything that is significant and visually powerful.

Tomorrow you will have a chance to use these objects to create your own altar of letting go.

Explore
- A quiet area of my home that would serve me nicely (for now) to create an altar of letting go . . .
- Someone or something that I am ready to let go of . . .
- Objects that I can use to help me let go . . .

DAY 264
LETTING GO ALTAR AND RITUAL

Today (or sometime this week when you can manage an hour of alone time), I invite you to create an altar of letting go. This intentional exercise is powerful when you give it all of your attention.

A quick word about altars: It does *not* have to be a big, fancy deal. You do not have to have a beautiful, pristine, clear space for it to work its magic. All you need is a focal point—a little place that you declare sacred to you. As you become more connected to your altar, it will change . . . and so will you!

1. **Place a small table or shelf** in a quiet area of your home where you can imagine spending a minute or two every day.

2. **Add** a colorful cloth, flowers, a candle, plus any objects that make your heart sing.

3. **Gather items** that symbolize things, people, habits, beliefs, painful memories, or outcomes you wish to release (e.g., clothing, letters, food, photos of an ex . . .)

4. **Light a candle**, close your eyes, and take a moment to center.

5. **Call in** a divine presence or higher power to hold a space for you and help anchor your intentions.

6. **Expand** your energy field with your breath, and imagine it filling the room as you repeat this blessing silently or out loud: "May this (thing, thought, aspect of myself, painful memory, relationship) be fully released for the highest and best good of all concerned. And so it is. And so it shall be."

7. **Allow** yourself to feel all sensations or emotions that arise without fixing, managing, or judging them. (This step is key.)

8. **Breathe**.

9. **Notice** in the days that follow any dreams, shifts, synchronicities, and aha moments and write them down.

10. **Maintain** your altar for as long as is required. Keep it fresh and vibrant; replace objects regularly, and move your altar (or remove it altogether) if it isn't working for you.

Explore

- I am ready to ritually release . . .
- When I set an intention, call in a higher power, and surrender to the moment, I notice . . .

DAY 265
LETTING IN, LETTING GO

Take a moment today to revisit and reflect on the challenging issue or unsupportable relationship that you identified and worked with in yesterday's lesson.

Stand in front of your altar and follow steps 3 through 7 in yesterday's ritual of letting go.

Note: If you don't yet have an altar, do the exercise anyway. Come back to this lesson when you have an altar too.

Explore
- It is safe for me to let this go now because . . .
- One thing I can do to support and honor myself now is . . .

DAY 266
CHECK IN—HONORING THE PAST

The focus this week was to remember in the best sense of the word: to gather, mend, and honor the scattered parts of ourselves with intention, action, non-identification, and compassion. Altars offer an excellent way to integrate and combine these four pathways of clearing.

In what ways does having a focal point help you to let go and feel more connected and spacious?

Explore
- Some of the things (people, situations) I have honored this week . . .
- Honoring my past has helped me feel . . .
- One way I can refresh my altar today is . . .

WEEK 39
CULTIVATING DEEP REST

I wish I could show you,
When you are lonely or in darkness,
The Astonishing Light
Of your own Being!
>—Hafiz, "My Brilliant Image," *I Heard God Laughing*,
>Translated by Daniel Ladinsky

DAY 267
ARE YOU FEELING THE BLUES?

Is it true that women today are in a funk?

In her blog post entitled "The Sad, Shocking Truth About How Women Are Feeling," Arianna Huffington writes the following:

> According to study after study, women are becoming more and more unhappy. This drop in happiness is found in women across the social and economic landscape. It doesn't matter what their marital status is, how much money they make, whether or not they have children, their ethnic background, or the country they live in. Women around the world are in a funk.

The subject of women "doing"—taking on too much, having no space for themselves, facing an empty nest, forgetting what makes their heart sing, yearning to connect more deeply (in ways they were designed to connect)—touches on many levels for me.

Let's open this conversation, shall we?

Explore

- I believe that women are more (or less) happy now because . . .
- I am more (or less) happy now because . . .

DAY 268
WOMEN WEIGH IN

Are you happy?

This is not a yes or no question. Hidden in there, begging to be revealed, is the *why*.

When I asked my readers to weigh in on the subject of personal fulfillment, their varied and thoughtful responses could have filled an entire book. Clearly, becoming oneself is a work in progress. Here are a few examples:

> I sometimes feel that I can't remember what it's like to just be "me." Don't get me wrong, I love my husband and the kids, but sometimes I'd like to remember what it's like to be me. (Kim)

> The blues went away when I began to honor my long-postponed dream/desire/obsession with going back to school to finish an interrupted bachelor's degree. Amongst the "doing" I came across ideas, concepts, traditions, and ground-breaking news in various fields that ignited my soul, spirit, and intellect . . . in other words, my entire being woke up. (Nancy S.)

> I think feeling blue and over-extended has always been with us . . . and while it may not be comfortable to look at, there is something positive going on . . . As we change how we relate to these feelings and experiences, with awareness and compassion, happiness has a way of simply emerging—it's right there. (Karen J.)

Care to weigh in?

Explore

- When I feel blue or overextended, I . . .
- What I can see changing for the better . . .

DAY 269
DEPRESSED OR DEEP REST?

Depressed or deep rest? I love how the pathway to healing is implied in that question—like the Young Girl–Old Woman illusion drawing. Your perspective determines what you see and experience.

Martha Beck, life coach and best-selling author, explains in *O, The Oprah Magazine* how "depressed or deep rest?" came to be:

> One day a client oozed into my office, slumped into a chair, and said she was depressed—only she said it so slowly that I thought she said "deep rest." In a way, this was accurate. Depression can be part of a general shutdown, meant to turn us toward healing. A tired body, a tired mind, a tired heart can't—and shouldn't—be passionate about anything but rest. So if you're exhausted, care for yourself.

Today, notice what is dragging you down or keeping you from moving forward. It could be a worrisome thought, an unresolved situation, a heavy heart. See if simply being aware of your resistance releases it—and you.

Explore

- Something that is dragging me down or keeping me from moving forward is . . .
- When I insert compassionate awareness, this happens . . .

DAY 270
REST MEDITATION

Today, I invite you to deepen your experience of rest by practicing this simple exercise.

1. **Close your eyes,** and take a deep breath in and a slow, emptying breath out.

2. When you feel centered, **repeat the phrase** "I rest in stillness."

3. Just drop the phrase into your conscious awareness—like a pebble in a still pond. **Notice and allow** the thoughts, emotions, and physical sensations that ripple out naturally . . . "I rest in stillness."

4. You can **repeat** the same phrase or go on to the next one: "I rest in awareness."

5. **Imagine** that you are dropping another pebble in the still pond as you go onto the final phrase: "I rest in awareness."

6. When you're ready, **move to the final phrase:** "I rest."

7. **Repeat** the phrases even if your life doesn't feel restful— especially if it doesn't. Every time the mind chimes in with all the reasons why rest is not possible, say it again. And again.

8. When you feel complete, **open your eyes** and bring your awareness back to your more rested self sitting in the room.

9. **Notice** your breathing; notice if you're feeling differently now than you did when you began.

Explore

- Before the meditation, I was feeling . . .
- Deep rest feels like . . .
- Other ways that I experience deep rest in my life are . . .

DAY 271
CREATE A LANDING PAD

If you could use a soft landing right about now, a space to decompress, or a nesting spot at home to claim as your own, these gentle guidelines by Madisyn Taylor, cofounder and editor in chief of *DailyOM*, are an excellent place to start:

> Any space in which you find it easy to let go of stress and anxiety can become your landing pad. A basement or attic, spare room, or unused storage area, furnished with items that soothe you, can give you the privacy you need to unwind. . . . Remember to consider noise and activity levels while choosing the site of your landing pad. . . .
>
> The soft place to land that you create should inspire within you the mantra, "I can breath[e] here. I can relax here. I know I am safe here."

Can you think of a good place in your home that could serve as your soft place to land?

Explore

- A good place for me to land at home could be . . .
- It's a good landing pad because . . .

DAY 272
IN-TEND AND ATTEND

Consider this contemplation today:

> Directing your attention and allowing the feelings to arise without doing anything to fix, manage, or resist them automatically changes the energy in the space.

For Withpaint, this concept of non-doing and not identifying (that has been slowly "dripping" into her clearing experience) has resulted in a big aha:

> Two weeks ago . . . I was feeling completely disconnected from my marriage. Just allowing those feelings to be was what helped me to question what was going on in me without judgment.

> Somehow this process of seeing them as interesting notes or symptoms . . . being aware and taking note as an observer . . . somehow changed how I experienced them . . . more of an observer . . . less of a victim to them. Don't know if that makes sense . . . but it was a paradigm shift for me. I could be forgiving and accepting of what was going on in me . . . and not become stuck.

> I was able to tell my husband what I was feeling without blame . . . just how I was going through some weird stuff. Later I realized it was fear-based . . . fear of aging . . . fear of getting older-looking . . . fear of the unknown.

> Not getting mired down in self-hate or anger . . . but letting the feelings become a signal for me . . . a sign of something amiss within . . . allowed space for me to see the underlying issues a lot better.

What is one thing in your home or life that could use a little redirecting?

Explore

- One thing that could use some redirecting today . . .
- What it feels like to in-tend . . .

DAY 273
CHECK IN—CULTIVATING DEEP REST

The focus this week was to shine light on overdoing and burnout as a cultural pattern and explore the effects it has on our spirit. Taking time to restore and renew ourselves through deep rest is as important as eating and breathing.

How does it feel to cultivate deep rest? What ways have you found to take guilt-free time for yourself? Have you created a "landing pad" at home? Are you using it? If not, what is stopping you?

Explore

- The more I cultivate deep rest, the more I feel . . .
- These things stand in the way of getting deep rest . . .
- One thing I can do right now to pause is . . .

WEEK 40
GETTING GOOD SLEEP

The most basic shift we can make in redefining success in our
lives has to do with our strained relationship with sleep.
—Arianna Huffington

DAY 274
CRAWL INTO HEAVEN

If I've learned anything at all after years of clearing, it's that letting go is
not possible unless we feel safe. And one of the simplest ways to create a
nesting place where we can be cozy, rest deeply, and feel safe begins with
the one thing we all need: a good bed.

My husband and I recently bought a new bed, and I adore it. Every
night feels like I'm crawling into heaven. I still can't believe how good it
feels to be so completely supported and nourished in this way.

Tell me, is there any reason not to feel like you're in heaven when you
crawl into bed every night?

Explore
- The thought of crawling into a heavenly bed makes me feel . . .
- What helps me feel most cozy and safe is . . .

DAY 275
ASSESS THE BED

To know if your bed is working for you, read the statements that follow out loud and notice how your body responds:

- I love getting into bed at night.
- I love the way my mattress supports every muscle in my body.
- I love the feeling of the sheets on my skin.
- My pillow supports my head, neck, and shoulders perfectly.
- I feel held and safe in my bed.
- I wake up feeling refreshed in the morning.

If each statement elicits a gushing, *Yes!* Congratulations! You got the bed thing down. Enjoy it!

If your reaction is one of desirous twinges or an aching body, it may be time to upgrade your bed experience. Use the prompts that follow to help.

Explore
- What works and doesn't work about my bed . . .
- One easy thing I can do today to change it up . . .
- One thing I can research this week to make my (our) bed work better for me (us) is . . .

DAY 276
THE BENEFITS OF SLEEP

Sleep—that delicious ritual that allows the body to rest is not just for refreshment. It turns out we need it as much, if not more so, for daily repair. There's a massive amount of cleanup going on in the brain while we're catching a few Zzzs.

Scientists have identified an "army" of cells in the brain called glial cells that clear out the toxic buildup of free radicals when the body sleeps. They're like our built-in night janitor doing the essential, thankless task of cleaning and restoring.

In her article for *Time*, "The Power of Sleep," Alice Park writes:

> Brain cells that don't get their needed break every night are like overworked employees on consecutive double shifts—eventually, they collapse. Working with mice, [Dr. Sigrid Veasey at the University of Pennsylvania] found that neurons that fire constantly to keep the brain alert spew out toxic free radicals as a by-product of making energy. During sleep, they produce antioxidants that mop up these potential poisons. But even after short periods of sleep loss, "the cells are working hard but cannot make enough antioxidants, so they progressively build up free radicals and some of the neurons die off." Once those brain cells are gone, they're gone for good.

You do the math. Less sleep means less cleanup of free radicals in the brain—which, according to research, increases the potential for serious degenerative disorders such as Alzheimer's disease, osteoporosis, and cancer.

If you're someone who can survive on very little sleep, or you've found strategies to stay awake longer, sorry to burst your bubble. The good news is, it's not too late to change course.

What is something you can swap out of your daily routine to take a refreshing catnap or log a few extra Zzzs? Your body will thank you for it later.

Explore

- Something I can swap out of my daily routine that I could replace with a catnap or downtime . . .
- One thing I can do right now to get some rest that my body will thank me for later . . .

DAY 277
REDUCE SCREEN TIME BEFORE BEDTIME

I can only imagine what life was like in the olden days—before electricity, when people went to bed at sundown.

No late-night adrenaline-rush episodes of *Homeland*. No text messages to check every sixty seconds. No cortisol-inducing social media to scroll, click, like, pin, share . . . Is it any wonder that we can't get good-quality sleep anymore?

We may not be able to turn back the clock, but we *can* reduce screen time before bedtime. Instead of checking emails one last time before turning in, how about reading a book? Or taking a bath? Or meditating?

You don't need to go cold turkey. Follow the Rule of One (see Day 54): Unplug one minute earlier than usual. Increase by one-minute increments each day.

Explore

- One thing I can substitute for screen time before bedtime . . . (Notice what the addiction feels like when you unplug.)

- What I notice in my sleep patterns when I give myself one hour (one minute) to unplug . . .

DAY 278
STEPS TO A GOOD NIGHT'S SLEEP

If you are someone who conks out the minute your head hits the pillow—without medication—and you sleep soundly until the next morning, you are blessed!

My nighttime rituals have become a top priority after learning about the consequences of sleep deprivation. Here are the steps I take to increase my chances of a good night's sleep:

1. **Take a hot shower** before getting into bed. It helps to release the stringy buildup of the day, it's calming, and it makes it easier to get into bed when it's cold out. Adding the Salt and Soda Refresh (see Day 257) to your shower or bath routine can be particularly useful here.

2. **Wear soft ear plugs**. I don't start with them in. I wait and see if sleep can prevail before reaching for them. If I'm awake after a half hour—conscious of the clock, my husband's breathing, and/or monkey mind beginning to stir— in they go. They seem to have a powerful pacifier effect, beyond blotting out sound.

3. **Meditate**. If I wake up inexplicably in the middle of the night (which happens less now because of the previous steps), I do not get out of bed to read. Instead, I coax my wakeful self to surrender to present time. Even if it does not

lead to instant sleep, it's refreshing, and helps to quiet the busy mind. Earplugs stay in.

Explore

- What helps me get a good night's sleep . . .
- When I can get a full night's sleep I feel . . .

DAY 279
YOUR RETREAT IS INSIDE

While we're on the subject this week of resting the body, here is a fitting quote from Marcus Aurelius:

> People look for retreats for themselves, in the country, by the coast, or in the hills . . . There is nowhere that a person can find a more peaceful and trouble-free retreat than in his own mind . . . So constantly give yourself this retreat and renew yourself.

The problems we face are not "out there." Whatever challenges you is not coming from some external source. If this concept feels farfetched and mystifying, would that be okay with you?

Explore

- I know that every challenge and solution begins and ends with me because . . .
- One small thing I can do today to go renew myself could be . . .

DAY 280
CHECK IN—GETTING GOOD SLEEP

The focus this week was to shine light on the importance of sleep, which, in the context of clearing, means way more than zoning out every night. Good sleep is powerful medicine: It allows the body, mind, and spirit to rest, refresh, repair, and remember.

How have your sleep habits and screen habits changed this week? Are you feeling more rested? What have you done to improve the quality of your bed and your sleep?

Explore

- How my sleep and screen habits have changed this week . . .
- What I have done to improve the quality of my bed and sleep . . .
- What I can still do to improve the quality of my bed and sleep . . .

WEEK 41
TUNING IN TO GUIDANCE

You have to leave the city of your comfort and go into the wilderness of your intuition. You can't get there by bus, only by hard work and risk and by not quite knowing what you're doing, but what you'll discover will be wonderful. What you'll discover will be yourself.

—Alan Alda

DAY 281
MAKE UP YOUR MIND

One Saturday, on the eve of my birthday, I had two wonderful offers: dinner with dear friends, and dinner with (other) dear friends.

How does one choose one fabulous opportunity over another?

On some level it was a no-brainer. One dinner had been planned in advance at a local restaurant we love and have been to a thousand times. The other was a last-minute invitation to the opening night of a brand-new restaurant in the city that specializes in scents. Yes, food and drinks that are designed to awaken all the senses, especially smell. How could I, with my highly developed schnoz, say no to such a wildly intriguing experience?

What to do? What to do? What to do?

Turns out, it wasn't that hard a decision when I was able to get out of my head and tune in to how I wanted to *feel*.

The thought of lights, glam, and lots of people was not a good match to the cozy intimacy and quiet conversation that my spirit needed most on that cold, rainy night. The choice became clear: Go with the original plan. Yes, even if it meant giving up on a once-in-a-lifetime opportunity. Celebrating my pre-birthday with dear friends we hadn't seen in ages at a quiet restaurant was exactly what I needed. Once the decision was made, I was able to move on without the slightest pang of regret.

When you let your feelings run ahead of your thinking, it's amazing how everything sorts itself out. It's funny, too, how "making up your mind" has nothing to do with the mind.

For the next two weeks, we will be exploring various ways to tap the part of us that *knows*.

Explore

- Next time I find myself at a crossroads of indecision, I want to feel . . .
- One thing that will help me remember to reach for that feeling when I need it . . .

DAY 282
YOUR INNER KNOWING

Belleruth Naparstek's description of the human intuition is so elegant. In her very readable and practical book *Your Sixth Sense,* she says:

> Because these occurrences seem to arrive unbidden and don't fit into our rationalist view of the world, we usually discount them or forget about them. But we're missing a big opportunity. Because with or without our conscious agreement, just below the surface of our lives, this boundless, abiding intelligence quietly sits and waits for us to recognize it.

We usually can't explain how we know, or measure how we know, or even prove how we know something. We just *know*.

The problem that usually arises, of course, is that we are too cluttered to know that we know!

Explore
- How I know that I know something . . .
- What helps me make a difficult decision . . .

DAY 283
FOLLOW YOUR KNOWS

Here's a quick and easy tool that I like to use when I'm stuck in my head and I can't decide whether or not to do something. It allows me to tap into and act from the place that already knows:

- If it feels right, do it.
- If it doesn't feel right, don't do it.
- If you don't know, wait until you know.

When using this tool to make an assessment, I've found it helpful to click an imaginary "quit" button on my thinking self before opening the feeling function of my knowing self.

Is there something that doesn't feel right (deep in your bones) that you could give some space to today?

Explore

- Something that doesn't feel right that I could give some space to today . . .
- When I have clarity about something, I feel . . .
- I know that I'm not in a clear space to decide something when . . .

DAY 284
WHEN IN DOUBT, WAIT IT OUT

It may feel counterintuitive, but there are times when it pays to wait out a dilemma.

For example, I once spent over an hour on the phone trying to sort out a fare impasse with an airline—getting bounced around in circles from agent to agent, from voicemail to voicemail. Finally, nearly ready to bag the trip altogether and erase all the progress I had made, I simply stopped trying. I hung up the phone and made dinner instead.

I decided not to decide.

In spite of the control freak part of me who can't stand leaving things unresolved for longer than two seconds, I did the unthinkable and walked away. You can imagine my surprise when I received a call the next day from a very friendly customer service representative confirming an even better fare and schedule! Recognizing that I didn't have the means to change the outcome at a particular moment in time resulted in my ultimate success.

It has taken me years to know when to back away. If nothing I do advances my efforts after a few tries, that is my sign to stop trying so hard and just *wait*.

How do you know when it's time to back away from a situation?

Explore

- How I know when to back away . . .
- Something that is bothering me that I could wait out . . .
  (Allow yourself to feel the resistance, or breathe into the need
  to control the situation.)

DAY 285
LOOK FOR PATTERNS

Writing this book has been an interesting exercise in surrender. When
I'm not sure what to say next or I hit a block, I'll stop and wait for my
next cue. It could be a word, a phrase, a story, a quote that I'll see in my
mind's eye. It helps a lot for me to be rested and in a quiet space (i.e., no
interruptions, no distractions).

How do you get information and guidance that you consider clear
and reliable? If you're a visual person like me, for example, it might come
in the form of pictures. If you're auditory, you might receive guidance
through sound. If you're kinesthetic, your signals might come through
physical touch or movement.

Use today to sense when your higher self sends you a clear message
and see if there is a pattern to it. Does getting a clear signal depend on
you moving your body, feeling rested, taking breaks, letting go of attach
ment to a particular outcome?

Explore

- Some of the ways I receive guidance that I can trust . . .
- What helps me get a clear signal . . .

DAY 286
WHAT CLEARING IS (AND ISN'T)

If I could boil clearing down to one truth, it would be this:

> We can only clear to the degree that we are in the present moment, have a clear intent, and have no attachment to the outcome.

If you're wondering why I've waited this long to state something so fundamental, it is because the truth of this statement would not have meant much in the early days of this journey. For it to sink in at a deeper, lasting level, this truth has to be practiced and *lived*.

Anytime you are focused on the past or the future, judge a situation as bad, and/or have an attachment to things being a certain way, *you are not clearing*. Nor making magic. When you find yourself in this situation, take a time-out and reach for the clearing mantra above. It is a space clearer's best friend: It cuts through a lot of internal red tape and lines you up to receiving guidance that is clear and reliable.

Explore
- I am not in the present moment when . . .
- One way to bring myself back to the present is . . .
- I know when I have a clear intent because . . .
- When I let go of attachment to an outcome, I feel . . .

DAY 287
CHECK IN—TUNING IN TO GUIDANCE

The focus this week was to adjust and tweak our internal antenna to help us connect with and receive guidance that is clear and reliable.

In what ways do you feel more aligned with the part of you that knows? How do you know *when* you're lined up?

Explore

- Some of the signals that my body gives me to indicate that I'm on track are . . .
- The best time of the day for me to tune in and trust my knowing is . . .
- What I know for sure is . . . (and why I know it . . .)

WEEK 42
IN-QUIRING

It is always with excitement that I wake up in the morning, wondering what my intuition will toss up to me, like gifts from the sea. I work with it and rely on it. It's my partner.
—Jonas Salk

DAY 288
BE CLEAR ON WHAT YOU'RE ASKING

Should I eat now? Does my body need food now?

You could say that both questions are asking the same thing—just framed in slightly different ways.

Not so. If you look more closely at the two questions and tune in to their phrasing, you may notice subtle distinctions. The first is more general, and it feels like it stops the flow. The second, more precise, question opens up to further inquiry.

What's the big deal, you might ask. Eating is eating.

If clear guidance is what you're looking for, posing the right question can be a game changer in space clearing. You may get a yes to eat now (as opposed to later), but a no if you're asking if your body needs food.

Welcome to my world of dowsing, where the questions really matter!

When I ask a yes or no question that is precise and grounded in details—name, time, and place—I get answers that come from a more clear and grounded place; answers that I can readily trust. And resting in the truth of an answer makes it much easier for me to detach from the outcome.

For example, "Should I clear my home today?" might deliver a very different answer than if I asked, "Is it the best use of my time to clear the bookcase today?" "Would it serve my highest and best good to clear the bookcase right now?"

Play with asking questions today. Pose them first in a general way, then rephrase them with specifics, and ask your higher self to deliver a clear answer through your six senses. Notice if the answer changes from one question to another, and if your internal "receiver" picks up the answer more quickly when you add details.

This week we'll explore a variety of ways you can play with questions to tap inner guidance.

Explore
- A general yes-or-no question I'd like to ask my higher self is . . .
- My question made more specific could be . . . (and what that feels like . . .)

DAY 289
TURN YOUR DILEMMA
INTO AN OPEN-ENDED QUERY

Yesterday we looked at the importance of phrasing a question to tap inner guidance. The creative mind is a fabulous problem solver. Give it something to chew on and it will take you to surprising places.

I find that asking my higher self to deliver guidance works much better if I turn my question into an open-ended query. The open format is a great way to tap inner wisdom and jiggle loose what gets in the way—especially when you're willing to wait for answers to reveal themselves.

If it's a query about how to best use your time, you might pose something like this: "One task that would help me feel most productive this morning is . . ." or "One quick thing I can do that would help me feel lighter (clearer, calmer) right now would be . . ."

If it's a bigger question about a life direction, for example, say, "One small step I can take today toward uncovering my life purpose is . . ." or "One small thing I can do that would help me gain some clarity in this situation is . . ."

If it helps move things along you can imagine your heart and mind opening up like a receiver. Invite the clearest information to flow into you in a way that you can understand and process.

The important thing with any question you pose is that you be receptive, and go for the feeling of an outcome as much as possible.

Explore
- A question I would like to ask my higher self is . . .
- How I want to feel when I've resolved this dilemma . . .

DAY 290
BURNING QUESTIONS

Burning questions are those time-sensitive queries that require an answer sooner rather than later. Should I say yes to the job offer? Who should I call to help me with my taxes? Should I see a doctor about this strange mole on my arm before I go on vacation?

What usually helps me to jiggle an answer loose is walking. There is a specific bend in the road of my usual walking path, about a block away from my house, where I often receive some clarity about an issue that has eluded me all day.

I also generate a lot of ideas in that dreamy state just before getting out of bed in the morning, or when I'm practicing yoga. I'll clear many mental cobwebs when I'm sweeping, or meditating. Some of my best book ideas and chapter titles have actually come to me while I've been soaking in a hot bath.

No matter what the question is, or what form it takes to arrive at a clear answer, it helps a lot if the question being asked is super clear.

Explore
- A burning question I have is . . .
- One thing I can try to do to resolve it is . . .

DAY 291
WONDER QUESTIONS

So far we've mentioned the idea of wonder questions a few times. Today, this is going to be our sole focus.

In her poem "Have You Ever Tried to Enter the Long Black Branches," Mary Oliver writes, "Listen, are you breathing just a little, and calling it a life?" This is what I would call a wonder question. A wonder question is not meant to be answered in a traditional way. It is meant to be imbibed, cultivated, lived. With full awareness and heart.

Because answers to wonder questions have a way of coming through in the smallest whispery details, it helps to pay attention to all signs: from the universe, Nature, synchronicities, impulses, aha moments.

What is a wonder question that you could pose? What are some answers that have begun to pop up to your bigger questions since you began this journey?

Explore
- A wonder question I could pose . . .

- Some answers that have begun to pop up since I began this journey . . .

DAY 292
MUSCLE TESTING
FOR GUIDANCE—PART I

If something doesn't feel right deep in your bones, it is probably wise to listen. The problem comes when our systems are so flooded with noise and overwhelmed by static that nothing we do yields any clarity. One of my favorite ways to bypass the monkey mind is a form of dowsing called muscle testing.

Based on the fundamental principle that the body knows what it needs and what's best for it, practitioners of applied kinesiology use muscle testing to gain precise information about a client's food allergies, best healing treatments, or dosages.

Though I use it for healing purposes, muscle testing is a very practical tool for daily decision making as well. It comes in handy, for example, when determining how many jalapeños to put in my soup, or when I'm picking a wine out of hundreds at the store. I'll muscle test titles of blog posts, or word phrasing, when I'm feeling stuck in my writing.

Is there a dilemma you are facing today that could be addressed with a simple yes or no question? What happens when we wait for the answer to be revealed and let go of attachment to the outcome?

Explore
- A dilemma that I'm facing . . .
- Some simple yes or no questions I could pose to help see me through this dilemma might be . . .
- When I put out the question, wait for the answer, and let go of attachment to the outcome, I notice . . .

DAY 293
MUSCLE TESTING
FOR GUIDANCE—PART 2

It is easy to muscle test yourself when you are in need of an answer that might directly benefit or affect you and others. All you need to do is ask a specific yes-or-no question and allow your own body's wisdom to guide you. Try the steps that follow.

There is one caveat: The tool will not work if you are attached to a particular outcome. It's easy for our desires and preferences to cloud the signals that our body receives and gives.

1. **Press your left thumb and forefinger** together to create a closed loop. Repeat with your right thumb and forefinger and interlock it with your left. When looped together they should look like two links of a chain.

2. **Keep a firm but gentle lock with both thumbs** and forefingers when stating a yes/no question. There should be resistance when you try to pull the interlocking loops apart.

3. To **learn your own body's code**, say quietly to your self, **"Show me a yes,"** as you gently tug the two circles apart. If the seal holds its tension, this will be the indicator of your true yes. If it can easily be broken, then the latter will indicate your body's yes response.

4. **Repeat** the exercise with the phrase **"Show me a no."** This should yield an opposite (or different) response to your yes. (*Note:* There is no right or wrong answer here. My true "yes" loop-hold, for example, remains strong and tight, while my "no" feels weak, slippery, and tends to break apart.)

5. You can **further test** your body's yes/no response with other true/false statements that are clear and unequivocal:

E.g., "I have ten fingers," "I live in Oakland," "I was born in 1963." With a few practice rounds you'll get a better sense on how your body delivers its feedback.

6. **Keep in mind** that you can ask any yes/no question provided that you are not attached to the outcome and you state your questions clearly. For example, "Should I take the workshop?" might give you a very different answer than if you asked, "Should I take the Business Strategies workshop?"

7. You can **fine-tune your query** by asking additional questions, such as: "Would it serve my highest good to take the Business Strategies workshop?" "Is this the best time for me to take the business workshop?" "Is there another workshop that would serve me even better in building my career?" The key is to be as precise as you can with your questions.

Note: Do not use this tool to make a major decision that could be potentially life-threatening. It is very difficult—almost impossible—not to be attached to an outcome when the health and safety of a person you know and love is at stake.

This is a powerful tool. Be as quiet and detached when you pose a question and trust your body to deliver guidance. It will take some practice to get the hang of this process if you've never done it before.

Explore

- My "true yes" loop-hold feels . . .
- My "true no" loop-hold feels . . .
- Some yes/no questions that I can play with to strengthen my muscle-testing skills are . . .
- Some yes/no questions that I can apply to what I have been noodling on over the past couple of days . . .

DAY 294
CHECK IN—IN-QUIRING

The focus this week was to use inquiry and wonder to bypass the monkey mind and tap the clear place within ourselves that knows the answer. It's easy for our desires and preferences to cloud the signals that our body receives and gives. What we learn when we practice self-inquiry is that the body and the heart never lie.

Did you notice if certain places or circumstances were more likely to reveal guidance, or some kind of clear signal about your next steps, than others? What are your clues that you are on the right track? How do you know that you know?

Explore
- A form of self-inquiry that has helped me gain greater clarity this week is . . .
- A dilemma that I would like more clarity around is . . .
- Receiving clear guidance feels . . .

WEEK 43
EMBRACING
NOT-KNOWING

If you understand, things are just as they are; if you do not understand, things are just as they are.
—Zen koan

DAY 295
NOT KNOWING

Some of you may remember what life was like in your early twenties. You've left home (or hope to), and you're preparing to take those first awkward steps of forging your own path as a young adult, full of hope and expectation.

This email my husband and I received from our newly minted college graduate daughter after a job interview is as good a summary as any of what these spells of unknowing can feel like:

Feeling unexpectedly exhausted after that interview. I have been mentally preparing for so long. The two hours passed in the blink of an eye and before I knew it, we were shaking hands and the waiting game began once more.

I just can't believe I still don't know what my next step will be.

Finding our way in the world is no easy task, no matter how old we are. The roller coaster ride can hit at any age. There's no manual for how to make a living or a life that feeds the soul.

Here's how I replied to our daughter that day:

Hi honey, my two cents: All good.

The waiting game is something we have become very accustomed to living here in Mexico: waiting for the plumber, waiting for an estimate, waiting in line at the bank, and then waiting for internet to come back on, or electricity . . . waiting and waiting . . . where nothing is going as planned . . .

And then suddenly something unexpected and magical happens, or someone shows up a day early, and you are pleasantly surprised.

This fuzzy-time of not knowing is excellent preparation for life. By the time you land somewhere you will have developed a really solid go-with-the-flow muscle that will stand you in really good stead.

Keep living your life with joy and passion, sweetheart. That's all you can do. Be present to what is happening right now, knowing that something will eventually shake your way.

With the life experience that you have cultivated so far, what would you tell your younger self about how things will work out?

Explore
- One thing I would tell my younger self . . .
- One thing I know for sure . . .

DAY 296
WHEN NOTHING HAPPENS

So what happens after you've set your intentions and indicated strongly to the universe that you are all in, yet nothing happens?

The waiting game is fraying your resolve, frying your circuits, and making you go crazy with not knowing. With that much time and wondering, the mind can play some crazy games.

Hang in there. Not knowing can be a very fertile place to hang out if you can bear the discomfort of it.

Explore
- Something I have been waiting for for a long time . . .
- Why I know that it is worth waiting for . . .
- What I can do to cultivate the trust that things will work out . . .

DAY 297
SURRENDER TO MYSTERY

Dark and messy, not knowing has a spectacular way of rattling our cage. Humans don't like how it feels to steep in gray area. It feels like a big mistake, a freak of nature. We mistrust it.

Here's the thing: Not knowing is a legitimate state of being. It's as valid a place to be in as certainty, clarity of purpose, and deep knowing.

Not knowing does not mean not caring. Staying present in this space for as long as it takes is a form of deep caring and requires patience. It is saying that you trust in divine intelligence—something larger than yourself—to sort things out.

Explore
- It is safe for me to hang out in a state of not knowing because . . . (Name and feel the part of you that doesn't feel so safe.)
- I know that things always work out for me—no matter what they look like on the outside—because . . .

DAY 298
EMBRACE YOUR NOT KNOWING

Is something happening in your life that doesn't add up, make sense, feels incomplete, is unresolved, or is downright mystifying? Are you noodling on something that you just can't figure out?

Today's invitation is to embrace the messy discomfort—*all of it.*

Take a few moments today to reflect on what it means and feels like to not know. See if by simply allowing yourself to not know moves enough energy to reveal even the tiniest peephole of clarity. Use the following prompts to help you.

Explore
- One thing I'm sitting with that mystifies me . . .
- One thing I can do to ease my discomfort around not knowing . . .
- When I hang out in that space, I notice. . .

DAY 299
LEAD WITH LOVE

Lead with love.

If you are wondering how that goes, here's a suggestion: Anytime you find yourself at a choice point (which is just about all of the time for most of us), simply ask yourself: Which way, Love?

And follow your "knows."

The heart knows.

Explore

- How I know that my heart knows . . .
- Where my heart is nudging me to go . . .

DAY 300
BE PATIENT

In 1903, when he was all of twenty-seven, the famous German poet Rainer Maria Rilke wrote a letter to an aspiring young poet. This particular passage from his book *Letters to a Young Poet* contains a universal truth that speaks to all of us. It is a terrific reminder on how to relax our need to know:

Dear sir,

Be patient toward all that is unsolved in your heart and try to love the questions themselves, like locked rooms and like books that are now written in a very foreign tongue. Do not now see the answers, which cannot be given you because you would not be able to live them. And the point is, to live everything. Live the questions now. Perhaps you will then gradually, without noticing it, live along some distant day into the answer. Perhaps you do carry within yourself the possibility of shaping and forming as a particularly happy way of living; train yourself to it—but take whatever comes with great trust, and if only it comes out of your own will, out of some need in your inmost being, take it upon yourself and hate nothing.

What big question are you *living* now?

Explore

- The question I am living now is . . .
- What would help me to cultivate more patience . . .

DAY 301
CHECK IN—EMBRACING NOT-KNOWING

The focus this week was to consciously step into that messy nether-world that we all find ourselves in from time to time: not knowing. We explored how to wait things out and cultivate patience.

Have you become more comfortable hanging out in not knowing? In what ways do you feel more grounded in knowing that things always work out for you no matter what? What ways have worked to calm the part of the mind that needs to be in control?

Explore

- I am (or I'm not) comfortable not knowing because . . .
- Ways that I feel more grounded knowing that things always work out for me . . . (Notice the parts that don't feel so sure.)
- What it feels like to trust in something larger than myself . . .

WEEK 44
SUPPORTING REAL EASE

Oh, the comfort—

the inexpressible comfort of feeling safe with a person.
—Dinah Craik, "Friendship"

DAY 302
LOVE IS IN THE DETAILS

The other night when I crawled into our heavenly bed I noticed that my side had been turned down. Yes, like in those fancy hotels.

That would be my husband, who was already sound asleep on the other side. After thirty years of marriage I thought I had seen it all. This was a first. His unprompted gesture took my breath away.

Nothing had prepared me for how welcomed and supported I felt in that moment, awash in the love that was folded inside a simple diagonal of blanket and sheet.

It made me cry.

When have you felt most supported in your life? How did it make you feel?

Explore

- Times I have felt most supported . . . (and how it made me feel . . .)
- Why I am worthy of love and support . . .

DAY 303
REAL EASE

I was teaching a class once when I inadvertently misspelled the word "release" on the whiteboard. Unthinking, I wrote "realease."

After a student pointed it out, I looked up and saw it: Real Ease.

Real plus ease equals release.

No mistake.

How does this formula apply in your life?

Explore
- How I know that real ease and release are connected . . .
- When I repeat the words real ease out loud, I feel . . .

DAY 304
WE NEED EACH OTHER

The famous singer Ella Fitzgerald once said,

> I owe Marilyn Monroe a real debt . . . She personally called the owner of the Mocambo, and told him she wanted me booked immediately, and if he would do it, she would take a front table every night. She told him—and it was true, due to Marilyn's superstar status—that the press would go wild. The owner said yes, and Marilyn was there, front table, every night. The press went overboard. After that, I never had to play a small jazz club again.

Yes, we long to connect. And we need each other. Now more than ever. Like the saying goes, "A rising tide lifts all boats."

Who can you ask for support?

Who needs "loving up"?

Explore
- Who I can ask for support . . .
- Who could use some loving up from me . . .

DAY 305
NATURE'S GRACE

Years ago while on sabbatical in Mexico, my family and I befriended an expatriate Swedish author. Though she was getting on in years and bedridden, Toni de Gerez was a spirited soul. She would regale us with stories of her amazing life as we sat enthralled by her bedside.

One of her lasting gifts to me was this one pearl of wisdom:

Teach me old woods to wither glad.

Her message is a beautiful reminder of nature's grace in the face of impermanence. If we're all going to grow old, why not have it be a class act? And why not let Nature, our best teacher, show us how?

What is something you can do today to honor and embrace your wisdom and life experience that you have cultivated over the years?

(PS The phrase originally comes from a hymn written in 1813 by the Danish poet Adam Oehlenschläger: "Teach me, O forest, wither happy." (*Lær mig, o skov, at visne glad.*) As best as I can tell, the "glad" adaptation—my favorite version—is Toni's.)

Explore
- One thing I can do today that honors my wisdom and life experience . . .

- How I feel about growing older . . .
- Ways that Nature can support me in aging gracefully . . .

DAY 306
THE CHAIR POSE

I practice a style of yoga every day called Svaroopa (pronounced *Swaroo-pa*). Based on a simple principle of "support equals release," it uses supported poses to release core tensions in the body and mind to promote deep relaxation and letting go.

The chair pose (my name for it) has a very specific purpose: to lengthen the spine and open up the tight muscles around the tailbone that cause us to feel tight everywhere else. It is especially good after long stretches sitting at a computer, long waits in airport lounges or doctor's offices, or after a very long and stressful day. Here's how to do it:

1. **Begin**: Sit in a sturdy chair, preferably one with no arms.
2. **Align**: Make sure that your thighs are parallel to the floor and your shins are perpendicular. To achieve the right angles if you are tall, place a blanket under your hips; if you are short, place a blanket or two under your feet. (*Note:* Keeping the thighs, legs, and floor at precisely right angles to each other prevents undue stress on the knees, back, and neck.)
3. **Position**: Place both knees shoulder distance apart, with heels directly under your knees, and feet pointed slightly inward. Make sure your big toes make firm contact with the floor.
4. **Adjust**: Slide your butt all the way back in the chair and place your elbows on your knees. Let your hands dangle freely.

5. **Move**: *Slowly* drop your head and hang over your knees like a rag doll.

6. **Tweak**: Tuck your chin in slightly to allow your neck to lengthen; adjust your upper back to create a hollow between your shoulders.

7. **Release**: Direct your breath along your spine, releasing holding areas, and let go.

8. **Finish**: To come out of this pose, place your hands one at a time on your knees or on the side of the chair. Come up *slowly*, one vertebra at a time, with your head last.

9. **Integrate:** Allow your body to integrate the effects of the pose by sitting quietly for a few breaths.

Try this pose for a few minutes every day and watch how this simple practice carries over into all aspects of your clearing life.

Explore

- What I notice in my body (and life) after doing the chair pose . . .
- When I am completely supported, I feel . . .

DAY 307
FIRST WORLD PROBLEMS

There's a very funny YouTube video by Ryan Higa that opens with the statement "Thousands of people fall victim to FWP [first-world problems]." With fake-sad music playing in the background, it features a handful of despairing twenty-somethings agonizing over their first-world problems:

I'm starving . . . all I have is . . . *leftovers* . . .

Nobody cares about me. Nobody commented or "liked" my status . . .

Why does Apple keep making new iPhones? Now I have to get another one!

The point of this video of course is to show how silly and small-minded our concerns can be sometimes.

So next time you're feeling overwhelmed, put upon, or caught in a "poor me" spin cycle, you might consider reaching for one of Higa's clever lifelines. If you're not too lost in your story, they will cut through the victim mentality and support release in a flash:

Here's a bridge; get over it.

Here's a straw; suck it up.

Here's a full cup; shut the full cup.

Isn't it nice to know that the universe has a way of delivering boundless (and humorous) options when we make room to receive them?

Is there anything that is bogging you down right now to which you could apply one of these lifelines? Do you recall a time when you had to "eat crow" and what it felt like?

If so, this would be an opportunity to bring compassionate awareness to any nudgy (or excruciating) discomfort that arises.

Explore

- A situation that is bogging me down is . . .
- Why it's easy (or not) for me to get over it . . .
- Sucking it up feels . . .

DAY 308
CHECK IN—SUPPORTING REAL EASE

The focus this week was to experience the connection between support and ease. When we feel loved up, safe, and supported we are more inclined to let go—to melt into spaciousness.

In what ways do you feel more supported this week? How easy was it to ask for, give, and/or receive support? How easy is it to face a difficult truth?

Explore

- Ways that I feel more supported this week . . .
- It is safe for me to ask for and receive support because . . . (Name and feel the part of you that doesn't feel so safe.)
- A difficult truth I am facing . . . (and ways to ease into it . . .)

WEEK 45
MARKING PROGRESS

Progress is impossible without change, and those who cannot
change their minds cannot change anything.
—George Bernard Shaw

DAY 309
BEING WITH NOISE

In 2004 my family and I moved to Mexico for six months. We each had different reasons for going. For our middle school daughter (at the time) the plan was to learn a second language while her young brain could soak it up like a sponge; for my husband it was to take a well-earned hiatus from his consulting practice and write; for me it was a chance to return to the land where I was born and raised, explore the cobblestone streets of my past, and speak Spanish again.

Sound like fun? Well it was. For *them*.

What I didn't expect was the huge amount of sensory overload and emotional baggage that would come with this package deal. I had created space in my life to explore, all right—explore *my resistances, my attachments, my fears.*

The sheer noise outside our bedroom window was enough to make anyone go mad—the tortilla factory clanking out thousands of tortillas, rooftop dogs barking at everything that moved, and construction workers throwing boulders into a truck at four o'clock every morning were just the warm-up!

For the first six weeks, I was in such resistance over the noise that I ended up nearly paralyzed with back pain. My circuits were fried. I was miserable. I was depressed. *What was I thinking? I chose this?!*

I felt like a junkie going cold turkey in rehab.

As Carlos Castaneda reminds us, "We either make ourselves miserable, or we make ourselves strong. The amount of work is the same." After those first few weeks of channeling (and releasing) misery, I came to a new place within myself by practicing not identifying with all the noise.

Having a really good set of earplugs helped a lot, too.

Explore

- A personal "dark night of the soul" experience I've had is . . .
- I processed it by . . .
- What it was like to visit a childhood home after spending years away . . .
- I know I am not my story because . . .

DAY 310
HOW SPACIOUS CAN YOU BE?

There are the obvious external clues of clearing success, an emptier bookcase, more white space in your email inbox, a new love interest, a job offer. But what about the internal markers? How spacious, detached, and present can you truly be when the next family reunion rolls around? Or a child becomes seriously ill? Or you feel misunderstood or deceived by someone you care about?

Are you able to glide about your life without as much as a button getting pushed?

This is what we'll be exploring this week.

Explore
- Where I feel spacious most of the time . . .
- Buttons that still get pushed in me . . . (and what it feels like to admit that they get me . . .)

DAY 311
FOUR LEVELS OF AWARENESS—PART 1

In the absence of someone shouting a progress report at regular intervals, here is a helpful model for assessing how far you've come with clearing. It's adapted from a theory called the Four Stages of Learning, attributed to the psychologist Abraham Maslow and used to explain how people learn new skills. For our purposes I'm calling it the Four Levels of Awareness.

Imagine the arc of any life challenge, such as going through a divorce, being let go at work, facing the death of a loved one, and divide the ways one might process and experience it into these four levels of awareness. Think of them not as a measure of how well you're doing, but how well you're *be*-ing:

- Level One: Unconscious Incompetence (no awareness)
- Level Two: Conscious Incompetence
- Level Three: Conscious Competence
- Level Four: Unconscious Competence (pure presence)

Don't let these cheerless, heady words throw you off. To the Western mindset, it is difficult to shake off the idea of competency as a measure of something other than "doing." Similarly, the word "unconscious" paired with "competence" at the fourth level can seem like a contradiction in terms.

This model is intended for no other purpose than to illustrate how we humans wake up, incrementally, to our true nature. The four levels indicate the spectrum of human consciousness, where zero awareness marks one end, and pure presence the other.

Tomorrow I'll explain each one in greater detail and show how they might apply to being more spacious and detached.

Explore
- If I were to guess the level where I spend most of my waking hours, it would be . . . (PS This is not a test.)
- What "be-ing" means to me . . .

DAY 312
FOUR LEVELS OF AWARENESS—PART 2

The Four Levels of Awareness model gives us a useful tool to mark our progress with clearing. Here's what each level of awareness means:

- **Level One: Unconscious Incompetence**—complete turmoil, uncertainty, chaos. At level one you feel helpless and overwhelmed. All your survival mechanisms are activated, and any clearing you do triggers stress hormones and resisting behaviors. You have no strategies in place to manage the chaos, and if you do have them, you're too overwhelmed to put them to use. At this stage it feels like there is no light at the end of the tunnel.
- **Level Two: Conscious Incompetence**—you begin to put one foot in front of the other. Your nervous system begins to settle down. You can see that the discomfort you are experiencing in your clearing is not who you are, yet you have no idea what to do about it. You are aware of your buttons getting pushed but have no resources, strategies, or practice tools in place to manage the bumpy weather when it comes up. It feels like there is a peephole of light at the end of the tunnel.

- **Level Three: Conscious Competence**—competency. At level three you know what it feels like to let go (with intention, action, non-identification, and compassion), but it takes conscious effort to cultivate it. You recognize the places you hold on and know that you are not a victim of your circumstances. You feel a greater sense of ease and possibility and know that hope is possible. The tunnel is filling with light.
- **Level Four: Unconscious Competence**—pure awareness, effortlessness, spacious detachment, mastery. At level four you are in the spacious zone: You are able to let go with an open heart without even thinking about it. You don't fix or judge. You take nothing personally. You accept things as they are. You laugh a lot. You vibrate clarity and attract people, places, and opportunities that are a vibrational match. You clear by just being a witnessing presence. At this level of awareness there is no tunnel; all is brilliant, shimmering light.

When you began this journey over three hundred days ago, where would you place yourself on the spectrum of awareness? And where do you find yourself spending most of the time now?

Respond to the following prompts in your journal to help you assess your progress.

Explore
- Unconscious incompetence would describe the part of me that is still . . .
- I know I'm at the level of conscious incompetence when . . .
- The side of me that shows up as consciously competent in my life is . . .
- Where I most excel and I consider myself masterful would be in . . .

DAY 313
CAN YOU ALLOW?

Here's a wonder question for you to consider today:

If you could let go completely of what's holding you back, would you do it?

Letting go. It could be that easy. If we allowed it.

Explore
- I can allow . . .
- What is hard for me to allow . . .

DAY 314
MEANINGFUL MARBLES

On a scale of 1 to 10, how is your day going so far? Has it been memorable? Exciting? Meaningful?

On her blog *Life by Me,* Sophie Chiche describes a simple and elegant ritual she uses to evaluate, mark, and celebrate a life that has meaning. It involves a bowl of several thousand marbles to equal one a day for (a self-selecting) period of twenty-four years.

Chiche's daily practice is to take one marble out of the bowl and place it in another bowl if she feels that her day has been meaningful. If she does not feel connected to something that gave her meaning that day, the marble goes in the trash. She writes:

> Tonight, I'll make a commitment to my friends that I'll attempt to live my life so that I move every marble to the other container and not to the trash.
>
> Trash is for banana peels and yesterday's paper.

Meaning is for everyone. Meaning isn't just for birthdays. It's for every day.

I think this marble exercise could work quite nicely as a daily check-in and celebration of your baby-step progress in clearing and self-care. What do you think?

Explore

- On a scale of 1 to 10, my day is going . . .
- What I find meaningful in my life that I want to cultivate more of . . .

DAY 315
CHECK IN—MARKING PROGRESS

The focus this week was to apply some tools to help us assess how well we're "be-ing" (versus doing) in our journey of clearing and awakening.

What have you learned most about yourself this week? What are some of your biggest strengths with regards to letting go, and what continues to be challenging for you? How spacious and detached can you be when life throws you a curve ball?

(If you feel a little nudgy weather creeping in right now, here's your chance to breathe into it now. This is not a race and there is no finish line.)

Explore

- When I began my clearing journey I was at level . . .
- Now, I feel I'm at this level . . .
- One thing I can do to expand my level of awareness is . . .
- One of life's recent curve balls was . . . (and this is how I handled it . . .)

WEEK 46
BEING WITH LOSS

The [dove] that [remains] at home, never exposed to loss,
innocent and secure, cannot know tenderness.
—Rainer Maria Rilke

DAY 316
THE EYE OF THE STORM

How do we allow a loss to simply *be*? To allow that things sometimes don't work out, make sense, or add up?

This wonder question was triggered a few years back when my beloved laptop crashed and I thought I had lost everything. Here's what I wrote that week:

> I'm still in shock and recovery over the fact that my laptop crashed last week. All emails, all photos, and who knows what else. Gone.

> It's not just a computer that has put me over the edge of unbearableness. I'm also still drying out and clearing the damage from a major flood in our basement, and consoling a majorly bummed-out daughter who didn't get into some of her top choice colleges . . .

> I'm not complaining, mind you. If anything, I feel profoundly grateful. Next to the death of a loved one or a pet, or a Hurricane Katrina-type loss, these events are small potatoes. Our house is still standing. I have my family and my health. Computers are replaceable.

I'm just allowing myself to breathe into the cumulative impact of what feels like a train wreck. To "stay with the initial tightening and not spin off," as Pema Chödrön wisely advises in one of her quotes that I love so much.

What I'm sitting with is *not* the why-me-why-now. I've learned the hard way that those kinds of questions add no value.

What I'm wondering is: How is it possible to remain spacious and detached in the middle of a crisis—to be the "eye," not the storm?

(. . . I just heard the word . . . "*Breathe*!")

Here's how it played out in the end: My laptop made it through and I recovered everything; our basement is a hundred times better now (aka clearer); our daughter got into the perfect college, had four amazing years, and graduated with high honors.

Yes, I would say in the end it was: all good.

Explore

- A crisis that I experienced in my past . . . (and how it turned out . . .)
- What I know now as I look back on that moment . . .

DAY 317
IT'S NOT ABOUT GETTING RID OF

Clearing is not about getting rid of.
It's not about getting rid of things.
It's not about getting rid of worry.
It's not about getting rid of pain.
It's about *letting them go.*

What are you ready to let go of now? What have you released already that you can acknowledge and be proud of?

Explore
- What it feels like to get rid of . . .
- What it might feel like to let it go . . .
- What I have released over the course of this year that I am proud of . . .

DAY 318
LOST AND FOUND IN LETTING GO

How does the mind deal with loss, and what does it take to experience a peaceful resolution? This beautiful letter I received from a reader illustrates monkey mind to perfection. Thank for this, Beverly R.:

Learning spacious detachment was forced upon me this past summer. I was thrust into a situation within seconds . . .

The situation? The passing of my mother.

Although things happened really fast, we had been preparing for this time for over a year, so it really was not a surprise to any of us, but the swiftness of the moment still took us all by surprise, and then things needed to be done.

You can go, we will be ok—please don't go I am not ready for this—I have to be strong to hold up my brother, my father, my children—I need to get a list of people to call—I need to call people—I need to plan the memorial luncheon—I will make things my mother liked—I need to clean the house—I need to write a eulogy—I cannot speak at the memorial—I need to focus—I just need to get through the memorial . . . I just need to get through the memorial . . . I just need to get through the memorial.

An organized clutter of thoughts consumed me—pulled me through the fog of grief that had settled . . . and then the memorial was done. There was nothing left to organize, nothing left to do . . .

With the memorial over I sat outside, allowing the summer breeze to soften the thoughts of my mind . . . and as I sat my mind did go blank . . . no thoughts, no lists, just silence—it really was heaven.

In the (almost) eight months since my mother's passing, and with the heavy fog of grief lifted, I have visited that quiet space of no time on several occasions. Although the time spent there is not as long as it was the very first time, it is no less healing, no less glorious, no less heaven.

Heaven. Yes, it's always there, even when monkey mind is too caught up in noise to notice her presence.

Explore
- A loss that I am still processing (or have yet to process) . . .
- One thing I can do right now to cut myself some slack . . .

DAY 319
FROM SUFFERING TO OBSERVING

Just how do we get on with our growing when we're mired in stress and stuff? How do we keep our equanimity when things don't work out, make sense, or add up? How do we just surrender to accepting things as they are?

I have found a simple way to unhinge the part of the mind that has to know; has to fix; has to be right. It is one of the best tools I know on how to dis-identify and detach.

Two simple words: "This is."

When placed strategically at the beginning of a worrisome thought, "This is" can help you take a step back to release some of the charge and unplug from whatever is causing you pain.

For example, "I'm exhausted" becomes "This is exhaustion." "My feet are killing me" becomes "This is aching feet," or "This is foot pain." "I'm overwhelmed" becomes "This is overwhelm."

What is one thing that is bothering you right now? Add "This is" and you might just notice the weather dissolve like magic.

Explore
- One thing that is bothering me right now is . . .
- Some of the feelings that come up when I reframe with "This is" . . .
- What it feels like to suddenly become the observer of my discomfort or dilemma . . .

DAY 320
LET. IT. GO.

Let. It. Go.

Three little words that can change everything. Or, as Lao Tzu reminds us: "By letting go it all gets done."

What thought can you let go of right now?

Done.

Explore
- A thought that I can let go of right now is . . .
- Letting it go feels . . .
- Letting go can be as simple as that because . . . (Name and feel the part of you that doesn't believe it can be that simple.)

DAY 321
PARABLE OF LETTING GO

You've probably heard this next story about letting go. It speaks volumes to our human condition. Here's my paraphrased version.

Two Buddhist monks are walking in the forest when they encounter a beautiful woman in trouble. She is begging for help to cross the river, which is too wide, too deep, and too strong for her to manage on her own.

The monks come from a temple where the rules don't allow contact with women. They are not even allowed to speak to or look at them. (Notice your judgments here.)

Without hesitation the older monk walks over to the woman, picks her up, and carries her safely to the other side of the river. The younger monk is flabbergasted by this flagrant disregard of strict temple rules. *How could my elder dare to look at the woman, much less carry her in his arms?!*

The two monks walk through the forest in silence for awhile until the younger cannot take the torment any longer. He stops and exclaims, "How could you do that? How could you touch that woman?"

The elder stops, slowly turns around, and smiles at the young monk. Without missing a beat, he says: "Are you still carrying that woman with you? I put her down at the riverbank."

I heard someone say once that letting go a little bit each day helps us practice for the "big letting go" that we'll all face when we meet our maker.

What thoughts or worries would you like to put down now?

Explore

- Some thoughts or worries that I'm still carrying . . .
- One small thing I can do to release the grip . . .

DAY 322
CHECK IN—BEING WITH LOSS

Although the theme of letting go is a constant in this book, the focus this week was to put it front and center—through contemplations that invite us to shift awareness and personal stories that invite us to embrace deep loss. If you really think about it, each moment is an opportunity to let go, each out breath a kind of release. In the end, it is baby-step practices that help us to bypass our survival instincts and build a new muscle.

In what ways do you feel that you've grown your letting go muscle over the past months? What helps you remember that it is safe to let go?

Explore

- Ways that I have grown my letting go muscle . . .
- I know it is safe for me to let go because . . .

WEEK 47
FORGIVING

> I do not at all understand the mystery of grace—only that it meets us where we are but does not leave us where it found us.
> —Anne Lamott, *Traveling Mercies*

DAY 323
THE GRACE IN GATHERING

I start out kicking and screaming, and come home purring like a pussy-cat. Such is the summertime ritual of picking up our share of produce at the local community farm.

It takes no time to fall madly in love again with the simplicity of tromping through the fields: gathering flowers to make exuberant bouquets, picking raspberries (that rarely make it past the car ride home), feeling the smooth skins of chili peppers on my skin, being transported by the scents of cilantro and basil and mint.

Mostly what I love is the immediate calming effect that plants have on me. No matter what kind of day I'm having, it seems that I'm always brought back to my center; welcomed, embraced, nourished.

It's like this unassuming patch of land *knows* me. It doesn't care that I'm fried after a long day. Or that my hair is a mess. Or that the container I use to haul our weekly bounty is an old plastic laundry basket with broken handles. The land seems happy to have me back no matter what—willing to hold a space for me to regroup.

I'm at home here—at home doing this simple and ancient thing of gathering. Gathering food. Flowers. My thoughts. Gathering the parts of myself that have gone missing or astray.

It is this—the weekly communion of abiding love and forgiveness—that brings me to my knees.

Explore
- When I am deeply held, I feel . . .
- What forgiveness means to me . . .

DAY 324
HEART WORK

Forgiving—someone, something, ourselves—is one of the hardest things on the planet. I touched on this idea in *Your Spacious Self*, and I think it bears repeating:

> How does one reconcile the loss of a loved one? How does one justify the premature death of a child or the untimely death of a parent, sibling, friend, or pet? How does one wrap one's brain around the 9-11 insanity, the slaughter of innocent animals, the decimation of an entire ethnic group, the inexplicable horrors that come from natural disasters and human error?
>
> How does one forgive God, the universe, or whoever you want to blame for giving you an unsupportive spouse, an absentee parent, a hateful boss, an incompetent doctor, an unkind neighbor?
>
> The answer, from a humanly attached place, is: not easily.
>
> To have a heart so big that it can hold this much unbearable pain is advanced-level work.

Take a moment today to close your eyes and place your hands on your heart. Bring your awareness to this space and notice what it feels like to rest here. Imagine this area expanding with each out breath.

When you feel centered, thank her. Yes, just say "Thank you, heart." And breathe.

This is big work.

Explore

- When I bring awareness to my heart space, I feel . . .
- What it feels like to thank my heart . . .

DAY 325
FORGIVING IS CLEARING

Every lesson in this book has been building your heart muscle. Slow-drip practices in letting go and self-care is a form of forgiveness.

Every time you courageously face your fears, allow yourself to be vulnerable, or feel whatever you are feeling without judging it as good or bad, you are forgiving.

This is powerful stuff.

What or who are you ready to forgive today?

Explore

- I am ready to forgive . . .
- Why I must forgive . . .

DAY 326
DISSOLVE SELF-CRITICAL THOUGHTS

Someone posted this beautiful piece on Facebook that felt like something that I would write. It's called "How to dissolve self-critical thoughts," by Martin Soulreader. May it help you grow your heart muscle and forgive.

Notice them

Observe them

Don't react on them

The thoughts will scream at you for attention, hug them

Observe them

Love them

Dissolve them

This makes echoes of them

What are you ready to forgive in yourself?

Explore

- Something in myself that I'm ready to forgive is . . .
- It's safe for me to forgive myself because . . .

DAY 327
FORGIVE FOR YOU

If you're having trouble forgiving someone—feeling like if you do they'll somehow get a free pass and not have to take responsibility for their actions—here's a little spacious wisdom by Marianne Williamson that might help. I heard her say it in a movie in which she was featured called *The Shadow Effect: Illuminating the Hidden Power of Your True Self.*

> The universe will deal with that person's karma. You don't have to worry that if you "forgive them" that they're going to somehow live a deserved wonderful life . . .

> It is not just to make their day better, it is to free you.

Who and what are you ready to forgive today?

Take a few moments to consider this question. Allow all sensations to arise. Release attachment to your need for justice or to have things turn out the way you had planned, and just . . . let . . . it . . . go.

Breathe into this exercise every day and notice the changes in *you*.

Explore

- Someone I am ready to forgive is . . . (It could be you. Just sayin'.)
- An issue I am ready to forgive is . . .

DAY 328
FORGIVENESS FREES

There's no question we're all getting older. Every day we are faced with mortality (in a wrinkle-phobic culture where supple vigor rules).

Certain body parts aren't moving quite as fast as they used to? Sorry, you're over the hill.

Crow's-feet and gray hair? Step back, you're over the hill.

Can't keep up with lightning-speed changes in technology? Move over, slow poke, you're over the hill.

Are you an over-forty Hollywood actress? Sorry, the two spots reserved in this category have already been taken by Julia Roberts and Meryl Streep. Never mind that you're supremely gifted and experienced, and the world could use you as a role model. You're over the hill.

Ouch. I know. It's a jungle out there.

Our culture may be unforgiving, but you don't have to be. Age is a given, and Botox and body lifts can't compare to the ultimate freedom and flexibility that comes from forgiving yourself.

Here's what I want to know: Are you willing to forgive yourself now, to embrace the regrets of an unrealized or imperfect past and *move on* with what you came here to do?

Explore

- What didn't go as planned that I'm ready to forgive now . . .
- A regret that I'm ready to release . . .
- How I can make friends with aging . . .

DAY 329
CHECK IN—FORGIVING

The focus this week was to lighten our load through forgiveness. In a world of duality and polarization, forgiving is one of our biggest challenges.

How does it feel when you think about giving someone a pass? What would it take for you to let go of needing to be right or seeing justice served? What regrets, disappointments, and unrealized potential are you ready to forgive and embrace?

Explore

- Imagining giving someone a pass feels . . .
- What it would take for me to let go of needing to be right or seeing justice served . . .
- I am now ready to forgive myself for . . .

WEEK 48
SPACIOUS REVEALING

Just let it all go, and show me your spirit.
—Platon, portrait photographer

DAY 330
A WHOLE-Y MOMENT

While traveling in Italy to celebrate our twenty-fifth wedding anniversary, my husband captured a rare and unexpected photo of me with my eyes closed. I was enjoying a moment of quiet contemplation (before digging into a fabulous plate of homemade pasta).

It's a rare photo of me because usually I'm trying too hard to look good. *How's my hair? Is my lipstick on? Wait, this is my better side . . .*

In this photograph I see a stillness that I rarely get to witness in myself. I like it. I like how pure and uncluttered I look. I call it my holy moment.

Try it: Next time someone takes a photo of you, give yourself a second or two to breathe into the stillness within before the shutter clicks. Or take an un-self-conscious selfie and see what happens.

What do you look like when you let go of the need to be anyone other than who you are?

Explore

- When I'm in a place of stillness, I look like . . .

- What I see about myself that I've not noticed before . . .

- When I'm in a place of stillness, I feel . . .

DAY 331
SEE YOURSELF

Here's my invitation to you today: Find a photograph of yourself that you are particularly fond of. Examine it closely.

What is it about this picture that moves you? What does this photo reveal in you that you haven't noticed before? Remember what Georgia O'Keeffe said: "To see takes time."

Explore
- A photo of me that I really love is . . . (because . . .)
- What this photo shows about me that I haven't noticed before . . .

DAY 332
MAKE A THOUGHT CLOUD

There's a fun website called Tweet Cloud that generates clouds out of the words you've used the most on Twitter during a select period of time. With a lovely calligraphic collage of your best (and worst) 140-character thought-bits you receive immediate feedback of what you've been putting out into the world. The greater the frequency, the larger the word.

It would be easy to adapt the same approach if you wanted a revealing snapshot of what's spinning in your headspace at any given moment in time. Here's how to play with it:

1. **Set a timer** for sixty seconds and write down on a big piece of paper every thought that goes through your head without censoring yourself. **Download** phrases, single words, repetitive grunts, random thoughts, brain farts . . .

2. **Notice** any squeamishness you have about writing down thoughts that are dark, uncomfortable, or "bad." Notice and allow the judgments to arise like clouds themselves.

3. When the bell goes off, **draw a big circle** around the words. There it is: your thought cloud for that minute.

4. **Try it again** at different times of the day—when you're feeling rested and when you're feeling tired, for example. Or when you're feeling serious and when you're feeling playful.

It's pretty daunting, really, if you consider how many unconscious thought clouds we generate in a day—especially the fear-based ones that don't evaporate as easily. Those are the ones to watch.

Just a thought. (*Wink*)

Explore

- What it feels like to download my thoughts without censoring them . . .
- Differences between thought clouds recorded at various times of day . . .
- What the thought cloud exercise reveals about me . . .

DAY 333
REVEALING LIGHT

Awareness is like turning on a special light switch that allows us to see more clearly our true, unplugged, unfiltered, spacious selves. I like to think of this light as being on a dimmer switch: The more we turn it up, the more we can see.

Our job with clearing is to turn up the light switch, slowly, and allow any and all information (as energy) to arise without personalizing or judging.

In his book *The Way to Love*, Anthony de Mello makes a similar invitation:

If you would only switch on the light of awareness and observe yourself and everything around you throughout the day, if you would see yourself reflected in the mirror of awareness the way you see your face reflected in a looking glass, that is, accurately, clearly, exactly as it is without the slightest distortion or addition, and if you observed this reflection without any judgment or condemnation, you would experience all sorts of marvelous changes coming about in you. Only you will not be in control of those changes, or be able to plan them in advance, or decide how and when they are to take place. It is this nonjudgmental awareness alone that heals and changes and makes one grow. But in its own way and at its own time.

What does it feel like to turn up the light on yourself? What do you see when you let go of judgment?

Explore
- When I turn up my inner light, I see . . .
- What is being revealed to me when I let go of judgment . . .

DAY 334
MIRROR EXERCISE

The steps that follow offer a simple way to raise your light of awareness. Try it for one minute sometime today when no one is around to make you feel self-conscious:

1. Find a quiet and private place to **stand alone in front of a mirror** for at least one minute. What do you notice?

2. **Allow your squirmy stuff** to come up without doing anything to fix or manage it.
3. **Notice your inner critic** piping in with any commentary about your appearance.
4. To the degree that you are able, **watch the thoughts** without giving them any importance or judging them as good or bad.

When the minute is up, notice how you feel.

Explore
- What I notice (and feel) when I stand in front of the mirror . . .
- How I feel now . . .

DAY 335
MIRROR MEDITATION

Today's practice is a variation on yesterday's mirror exercise. Give yourself some time for this and see if going deeper helps to release who you are not, and reveal more of who you are.

1. **Stand** in front of a mirror.
2. **Close your eyes,** and take a deep breath in and a slow, emptying breath out. With each out breath **repeat out loud**, *slowly,* three times to yourself: "Let it go . . . just let it go . . ."
3. Take another deep breath in and slow, emptying breath out and **say** out loud "Show me your spirit, (your name here)."
4. Keep breathing, and **allow the words to sink in**. Let the thoughts and feelings come and go. Tune in to sensations: smells, sounds, images.

5. When you feel complete, **open your eyes** and notice what you look like to yourself. Do you look softer or younger than you did before you started the exercise?

6. After you've had a chance to reflect in your journal, **repeat out loud**, "I exist. I matter. It is safe for me to show my true self."

What do you see when you open your eyes? What do you feel?

Explore
- This mirror meditation reveals about me . . .
- Saying "I exist. I matter," feels . . .
- Why it is safe for me to show my true self . . . (Notice the parts of you that may not yet believe it.)

DAY 336
CHECK IN—SPACIOUS REVEALING

The focus this week was to shine the light of awareness on the aspects that we love about, and judge, in ourselves; to see what might be revealed when we look at ourselves more closely in a photograph, thought cloud, or mirror.

What does it feel like to shine light on yourself? How does "turning up the light" release what no longer works for you? For example, do negative thoughts lose their charge when you name and feel them?

Explore
- What it feels like to turn up the light on myself . . .
- How turning up the light releases what no longer works for me . . .
- Other revealing aha moments I've had this week . . .

WEEK 49
LOVING UP OUR SPACES

When you come in home here,

May all the weight of the world

Fall from your shoulders.
> —John O'Donohue, "For a New Home,"
> *To Bless the Space Between Us*

DAY 337
WELCOME HOME

Honey, I'm home!

One of my favorite TV shows growing up was *The Dick Van Dyke Show*. I never tired of watching Rob Petrie walk in the front door, put his hat and trench coat in the closet, do a playful quickstep around the ottoman, and kiss his welcoming doll of a wife, Laura, dressed impeccably in pearls and an apron. June Cleaver, the devoted mom in *Leave It to Beaver*, had a similar feel-good effect. What can I say? These people made me feel welcome. Safe. Loved up.

One-dimensional, white TV–fiction aside, coming home should feel good. We should all feel loved up in our homes. The problem is, we forget that our home can be a sanctuary. Maybe not "in pearls"—maybe a far cry from pearls, in fact—but nevertheless alive and dynamic.

We forget that the container we call home holds a space for us all day and night (not to mention all our stuff). When we focus on what's wrong with them—"the sink keeps clogging"; "the windows are filthy"; "there is not enough closet space "—we forget what is actually right with them. We forget that we're blessed to even have a home.

What is it about your home that you are most grateful for? This week, you'll have a chance to find out and "love her up"!

Explore

- What I love about my home is . . .
- What I am most grateful for about my home . . .

DAY 338
BATHE YOUR HOME IN LOVE

When my friend Nancy and her husband were building their house in Mexico, they wrote down a blessing on a piece of paper, placed it in a jar, and buried it in the ground before the cement trucks arrived to pour the foundation. It felt like a powerful way to set an intention and honor the place that would long outlast their time there.

You don't need to build a house and bury an invocation to honor your home. An appreciative blessing of any form is potent no matter what age, stage, or condition your place is in.

What is it about your home that you love? Take a moment today to write a letter and tell her. Tell her what you love about her and the specific ways she supports you every day.

As you write, imagine the words washing over (purifying, cleansing) your entire home and property inside and out.

Bathe her in love.

Explore

- Dear Home, what I want to say to you is . . .
- What it feels like to bathe my home in love . . .

DAY 339
HOMES ARE LIKE US

I've alluded many times to our spaces and houses being "alive," and just as people can become ill, our houses can get sick too. Since we can't give a house ibuprofen or an antacid, how do we help our home get better?

Our homes and workplaces are extensions of us. Through doorways and hallways, they circulate energy (chi)—or they don't, depending on how cluttered, congested, and gummed up they are. They expand and contract depending on the weather. They are affected by the land they sit on, neighboring properties, and yes, even the residue of memories left behind by previous occupants. Like people, our homes get stressed out, out of balance, even sick. But they also respond well to love.

How healthy is your home? What is one thing you can do today to nourish her? (PS The appreciative blessings you wrote in your letter to her yesterday are excellent medicine.)

Explore
- On a scale of 1 to 10, with 10 being super healthy, my home is . . .
- One thing I can do today to love her up . . .

DAY 340
LIGHTEN UP YOUR LIVING SPACE

Today's exercise is a great way to sparkle up a home, workplace, car—any space you occupy. This is an abbreviated version of the meditation I use with my clients at the end of a space clearing consultation to help them integrate the session.

Toward the end of this process, there will be an opportunity to place a "discerning field" around your space.

1. **Close your eyes**, and take an easy breath in and out.

2. **Put your hand on your heart** and ask to connect with the purest form of unconditional love and golden light radiating from the Divine or your concept of a higher power.

3. When you feel connected, **invite** this love and light energy to gently **infuse** and **envelop** your home (apartment, workplace, car . . .) until the space feels completely loved up.

4. **Ask** that this love and golden light energy act as a "discerning field," and that it hold for the highest good of all concerned for as long as is required. This invisible layer acts to filter out any negative influences that no longer serve your home, family, coworkers, and/or other occupants, visible and invisible. *Note:* the discerning field will not filter out that which is needed for your soul to evolve.

5. When you feel complete, **open your eyes** and notice what your space looks and feels like now.

Does your space look or feel brighter, or different, than when you began? How do you feel?

Note: Don't worry if you don't see or experience shifts right away. It may take a few days for the energies in your space to integrate to these higher frequencies. Look for subtle changes in ambient light continuing into the week.

Explore

- What it feels like to energetically "love up" my space . . .
- I've noticed these shifts since starting this practice . . .

DAY 341
LIGHTEN UP YOUR PERSONAL SPACE

It is easy to adapt yesterday's meditation to lighten the body's physical and energetic spaces as well. Placing a discerning field around yourself is an excellent way to establish clear, clean energetic boundaries with others. Once you get the hang of it, it works quickly to restore balance when you feel contracted, unsupported, small, or jangled.

Note: With any kind of energy work, be gentle with yourself. If at any point you feel inordinately tired, stop. Drink plenty of water, and practice extreme self-care. Give yourself time to grow the spacious muscle you need to do this powerful work.

1. **Close your eyes**, and take an easy breath in and out.
2. **Place your hand on your heart** and ask to connect with the purest form of unconditional love and golden light radiating from the Divine or your concept of a higher power.
3. When you've connected to your heart space, **invite** this love and golden light to gently **infuse** you with sparkling, healing energy until your entire physical body (cells, blood, organs, limbs, skin, hair—everything) feels completely cleansed and purified.
4. Once you've filled up your physical tank (so to speak), **beam** this clear, sparkly energy outwards, beyond your physical body, to infuse the subtle layers of your personal energy field, until it too feels completely cleansed, purified, and filled up (loved up).
5. **Ask** that this divine golden light and love act as a discerning field filter around your entire being—physical and energetic—for as long as is required.
6. When you feel complete, **open your eyes** and notice how you feel, beginning with your breathing.

What does it feel like to love yourself up this way? What does the world look like from this expanded place?

Explore

- What it feels like to expand energetically . . .
- What it feels like to allow heart energy to nourish me and lighten my load . . .

DAY 342
PLEDGE TO HONOR AND SUPPORT

Take a minute to consider one small way that you can honor, support, or bless your home every day for the next week and write it down in your journal.

When you feel ready, stand at the main entrance of your home and "expand out" using yesterday's lighten up process. Declare your intentions out loud beginning with this statement:

This week I promise to honor and support you by . . .

Notice any squirmy resistance you might feel around making a commitment in this way.

Explore

- What I promise to do this week that will honor and support my home . . .
- Ways that honoring my home honors me . . .

DAY 343
CHECK IN—LOVING UP OUR SPACES

The focus this week was to raise the vibration of our physical and energetic living spaces by inviting higher frequencies of light, love, and gratitude.

What are some of the shifts that you've noticed since you consciously began blessing and loving up the spaces you occupy? Have you noticed any subtle changes in the quality of ambient light in your home, for example? Do you feel more expanded in general? Is it easier to set and maintain clearer boundaries with others?

Explore
- Some of the shifts I'm noticing from consciously loving up my home and my self are . . .
- What has worked best for me this week to bring more light into my home and life . . .
- What can help me remember to connect with home in a more sacred way . . .

WEEK 50
DREAMING BIG

Tell me, what is it you plan to do

with your one wild and precious life?
—Mary Oliver,
"The Summer Day"

DAY 344
ANSWERING THE CALL

I am continually amazed by what can happen when we dream big: put one foot in front of the other, throw in massive amounts of chutzpah, and answer the call of a deep yearning in the face of not knowing.

I watched this play out in my own family two years ago.

For my husband it was a dream to walk the entire Camino to Santiago de Compostela. For years he'd talked about making the five-hundred-mile pilgrimage from France to the northwestern coast of Spain. He planned long and hard for it; saved money; told his clients he would not be reachable; packed (and repacked) his bag to get it down to a mere eighteen pounds; and, at the age of fifty-seven, made it happen. It took him five weeks to complete the journey.

For our then twenty-one-year-old daughter it was a calling to study in Paris and become fluent in French. Through sheer grit and determination she managed to squeak in enough language credits to get herself accepted into Sciences Po, one of the most selective and rigorous political science institutions in the world. Her dream to take high-level classes in French was audacious, especially given that just a year earlier her command of the language was zero!

What callings are bubbling up (or bursting forth) in your life? What life dreams are you ready to step into once and for all? What is your purpose here on the planet?

There are infinite ways to get unstuck and connect you to the stirrings of your soul. All you need is to start somewhere. And keep going.

Explore
- What is stirring in my soul . . .
- One of my life dreams is to . . .
- I believe that I am on this planet to . . .

DAY 345
DIVE IN

This message Anne Lamott posted to her Facebook page made me gulp:

> Oh my God, what if you wake up some day, and you're 65, or 75, and you never got your memoir or novel written; or you didn't go swimming in warm pools and oceans all those years because your thighs were jiggly and you had a nice big comfortable tummy; or you were just so strung out on perfectionism and people-pleasing that you forgot to have a big juicy creative life, of imagination and radical silliness and staring off into space like when you were a kid? It's going to break your heart. Don't let this happen.

Truth is, for most of my adult life I have held myself back from diving into delicious warm pools and oceans because of the "mess" that it would make of my hair. My *hair!* Unless my curly locks were in need of a wash anyway, I always chose looking good over feeling good.

What is keeping you from "diving into" that big, juicy life that is calling you forward?

Use your journal today to expand your awareness of a deep yearning (and "jiggle" loose what might be holding you back).

Explore
- One thing about me that I love and want to cultivate more of in my life is . . .
- A deep yearning I have . . .
- Ways that I hold myself back from embracing life with gusto . . .

DAY 346
CELEBRATE A COMPLETION

If something is holding you back from considering a big move, a life dream, or a fresh take on your purpose, it may be that you're still stuck in a previous chapter of your life.

If so, it may help to acknowledge, or celebrate, an ending. Ritual is a great way to honor your past, release the strings of attachment, and invite new beginnings.

If it's an empty nest you're facing, for example, you could create a beautiful ceremony where you graduate (with high honors) from active parenting. If it's an ex-relationship you're trying to move past, you can use your "altar of letting go" to say goodbye (see Day 264). Or you can draw a line in the sand and step over it to invoke a fresh start.

If it's emotional weather that continues to sock you in, or any issue for that matter, you can try this wonderful ritual that Jean came up with during her recent walk on the beach:

> I decided to pick up rocks along the way and think of them as obstacles to living the life of my dreams. So, I picked up ANGER and released it into the ocean (tossed the rock). Then I picked up

my need for CONTROL and released it in the ocean. I picked up my JOB and released it. I picked up FEAR and released it. I picked up my 50 pounds of excess WEIGHT and released it. I picked up DEBT and released it. I picked up junk food and released it. [Then] I picked up three pretty stones to bring home and write on and make a rock garden along with some others I have already collected. I will write: RELEASE, ACCEPTANCE, EMBRACE, LOVE, PEACE, JOY and the like. I felt so much joy, peace and beauty today. I felt lighter and freer.

Use your imagination. The unconscious mind doesn't know the difference between ritual and the real thing, so go for it!

What chapters in your life are you now ready to complete and celebrate?

Explore

- A chapter in my life that is over . . .
- One way I can celebrate and honor it and move on . . .
- How I feel now just thinking about letting this go . . . (Notice the part that doesn't feel comfortable yet with letting go and lean into it.)

DAY 347
EGO VERSUS SOUL

Author Elizabeth Gilbert was riding high from one of her speaking engagements on Oprah's "The Life You Want" tour when she posted this Facebook message describing the differences between ego and soul:

A woman asked [Pastor] Rob [Bell] yesterday how you can tell the difference between when your soul is talking to you, and when your ego is talking to you.

Rob started with an explanation of the ego, as a force that is never satisfied. Nothing will ever be enough for the ego—not enough money, not enough praise, not enough shoes, not enough Facebook likes . . . And when the ego DOES get something it wants (success, attention, a swimming pool), all it can do is crow about it.

Like: LOOK WHAT I DID!

Like: #KillingIt

As for the soul, though, all it wants is joy and light and love . . . and excitement. When you are living the life that your soul wants to live, you will wake up each morning and say, "Oh my god, I can't believe I get to do this today!" (Whatever "this" might be—write this book, work in this garden, live in this house, see this friend, eat this food, raise these children, walk in the woods with this dog . . .

Last night's dinner was a soul moment for me. I could not stop smiling. I could not stop hugging everyone . . . I could not stop thinking, "I can't believe I get to be here with these great and good people."

When was the last time you had a soul moment? How did your soul moment feel from top to bottom, inside and out?

Explore
- How I know when my ego is talking (versus my soul) . . .
- The last time I had a soul moment was . . . (and what it felt like) . . .

DAY 348
PLAYING SMALL DOES NOT SERVE

No one wins when we play small. I mean really. Holding back on our dreams, playing safe, and just settling with *whatever* benefits no one. Especially ourselves.

As Nelson Mandela once said, "There is no passion to be found playing small—in settling for a life that is less than the one you are capable of living."

In what ways are you still playing small? Close your eyes and just ask your heart. It knows.

Explore
- Ways that I am playing small . . .
- One small way that I can stretch myself today . . .

DAY 349
JUST IMAGINE

Start today by considering this question from Lena Stevens, which she posted on her blog, *The Power Path*:

> What if this path you are experiencing now will take you forward into a life so magical and fulfilling that you cannot even imagine it?

Ooh yes! Can you feel it? Doesn't the possibility of realizing your wildest imaginings sound giddy exciting?

Even if a life of magical fulfillment is not yet imaginable, the path itself certainly can be.

What is one (baby) step that would make you feel giddy excited?
Imagine *that*.

Explore
- What makes me feel giddy excited . . .
- One baby step that might lead to a place of magical fulfillment . . .

DAY 350
CHECK IN—DREAMING BIG

The focus this week was to connect with the stirrings of our soul: to honor deeper yearnings and imagine bigger dreams. We cannot truly step forward until we let go of what's holding us back.

In what ways do you recognize that you are way bigger and more powerful than you know? What might be holding you back from realizing your dreams? What does your heart know for sure?

Explore
- My soul is telling me . . .
- What is holding me back from stepping into a bigger dream . . .
- What my heart knows for sure . . .

WEEK 51
LOSING OURSELVES, FINDING OURSELVES

Not till we are lost ... do we begin to find ourselves.
—Henry David Thoreau, *Walden*

DAY 351
MORE YOU

With all the inspiration that I've received through life experience, extraordinary opportunity, and study with brilliant teachers over the years, there's no replacing the wisdom that simply comes from living life in present time, embracing the shadow when it shows up, and entering each moment with innocent curiosity. When I can bring these qualities to the table, I feel totally spacious—and complete.

You never know what spacious magic might be revealed when you put one foot in front of the other and clear the clutter of your life. As I wrote in *Your Spacious Self*,

> No matter what your clutter challenge is, as you practice clearing in this way, you'll begin to notice some shifts taking place in your life. Who knows what that might look like for you. It might start as a tiny peephole of space that wasn't there before. An *ah-ha*. A kindness. A quieter dog. A surprise check in the mail. Less junk mail. Fewer pounds. A job offer. Fewer buttons getting pressed. Better sleep. More energy. More joy.

> More you.

> More real, spacious you.

What can you see with greater clarity now since you began this journey almost a year ago?

Even if all you can see is your next baby step, you are golden.

Explore
- What I can see with greater clarity is . . .
- What I can see as a next step . . .

DAY 352
PURPOSEFUL IRRITATION

Like a freshwater pearl that begins as a simple grain of sand, we cannot become our shimmering, sparkly selves without some level of irritation.

Allow the irritations to come and go. Embrace them. Lean into them. Celebrate them, like Anne Lamott does here:

> At my church, we sing a gospel song called, "Hallelujah anyway." Everything's a mess, and you're going down the tubes financially, and gaining weight? Well, Hallelujah anyway.

And if you're still wondering why anyone would want to "feel into" anything that isn't pleasant, pose it to your higher self as a wonder question and allow the answer to reveal itself.

Explore
- What is still irritating me . . .
- What it feels like to lean into this irritation . . .
- Why I would want to "feel into" . . .

DAY 353
GROWING PAINS

It's no secret that clearing brings up "stuff." And the longer you've been holding on to stress and stuff, the more likely you are to feel some discomfort as you unwind from it. You might even feel worse, or less clear, than when you started. Yes, things can feel uncomfortable—even stuck or hopeless—for a while, as Karen G. posted recently:

> Working through the various layers in the beginning was not so hard, but now I am stuck. I have reached the layer of deep wounding . . . I thought I had begun to heal, but as I go through the clearing I am now feeling the naked truth of it all.

Before you throw in the towel, consider that each time you clear something you are peeling away another layer of issues (painful memories, shame, fear, loss)—that you could not even *feel* before because they were buried deep inside. Anytime you're feeling "under the weather," as it were, hang in there. This conscious discomfort is what I call growing pains. They are the pins and needles of waking up after holding on for an entire lifetime.

There is an addendum to Karen's comment above. Just one week after she shared her dark moment, she offered this:

> I am sitting here right now feeling love. My life with all the "stuff" feels hard and rocky. As I have shared, I am fighting the memories that turn into thoughts that hurt emotionally so much. I am getting better. But this morning, I feel love. This is a new feeling for me. I sit here alone, and feel love. Suddenly, all the clearing makes such sense. I do not want to share the pain today I want to enjoy this moment. Must begin [this new] day, but is this what it is about?

Yes, things can change (a lot), and today is a new day.
And yes, that *is* what clearing is about.

Explore
- Some growing pains I have been feeling . . .
- How I know that things are changing for the better . . .

DAY 354
SIGNPOSTS OF CLEARING

As with any journey, it helps to have markers to guide and assure you that you're on the right path. The signposts that follow will help remind you that you are doing just fine:

- **Feelings come up**—allow them.
- **Shift happens**—embrace it.
- **Outcomes change**—accept them.
- **Clarity comes into focus**—trust it.

Which of these have you noticed popping up in your journey? Which do you find most challenging? Which have you grown comfortable embracing?

Explore
- The signpost(s) that I am aware of . . .
- The signpost(s) that I've grown comfortable embracing . . .
- The signpost(s) that I find most challenging . . .

DAY 355
EVERY STEP MATTERS

No matter how small or seemingly insignificant your efforts may have felt to you in your clearing journey so far, *every step matters*.

Clearing even just one toothpick every day—with intention, action, non-identification, and compassion—leads to lasting change.

What is a constant that you've experienced this year?

Explore
- My life will always have . . .
- One way it can teach me constancy is . . .

DAY 356
A GENTLE REMINDER— STEPS TO STAYING ON TRACK

In this journey, where the focus is on clearing a lifetime of old patterning, it's very easy to get side railed and lose focus.

Next time you get discouraged or fall off the wagon into old habits, adopt these simple steps as a gentle reminder. They are designed around the Four Pathways of Clearing (see Day 9):

1. **Observe it:** Observe your energy levels go up and down without judging them as good or bad.
2. **Move it:** Consciously move something for at least a minute every day to create energy, momentum, and flow. You can sweep a floor, move a pile (e.g., laundry, dishes), put away something that is routinely out of place, do a yoga flow pose, take a walk—anything that is purposeful, fluid, and repetitive.

3. **Allow it:** Allow any discomfort or resistance to arise without taking it personally; the less attached you can be to any emotional weather, the quicker it will pass.

4. **Complete it:** Follow up any clearing task by doing one thing that feels good and makes your heart sing.

PS It might help to write these things down on a sticky note and place it in a visible location.

Remember that consistency is your secret weapon. Over time, intentional repetition of these steps will work their magic to uncover your true self.

Explore
- I know I'm getting side railed when . . .
- In addition to using the Steps as a way to bring me back to center, I would like to try . . .

DAY 357
CHECK IN—LOSING OURSELVES, FINDING OURSELVES

Clearing is a process of growing into and claiming our true nature and best life. The focus this week was to shine light on the growing pains and pitfalls that come with the territory; to remember that every baby step counts; and to recognize that changes—both comfortable and uncomfortable—are part of the journey back to wholeness.

What has this journey revealed about you? In what ways do you feel more connected and whole? And in what ways are you still growing?

Explore

- What is coming into focus for me . . .
- What I can lean into more . . .
- What I know for sure is . . .

WEEK 52
CONTINUING

The end is only the beginning.
    —Brian L. Weiss MD, *Miracles Happen*

DAY 358
SAYING GOODBYE

There is a word for it: *saudade*. It's Portuguese with no direct translation in English. It means a nostalgic longing for an absent something or someone. I don't know if it's used as a verb or a noun, but I'm feeling it. It may sound strange to say this, but I already miss you all!

I may not know you personally, but I know you through these pages. You are my sisters and my brothers—connected by a common desire to nourish our spirit and lighten our load. Through thick and thin we've gone far together.

And, still, you may be wondering: Does clearing ever end?

The "bad" news is that clearing never ends. The good news is that clearing never ends. When we can enter into the experience with wonder and spacious detachment is when clearing becomes a thing of beauty—a spiritual practice—that reveals the divine essence of who we are. Why would we ever want to stop doing that?!

No, the journey does not end here. In this last week you will have the opportunity to reflect on how you've changed, and you'll also receive some goodies to help you stay on the path for years to come.

Explore
- How I know that clearing doesn't end . . .
- I trust myself to keep going because . . .

DAY 359
YOU'VE CHANGED!

One of the many things I've learned about this journey is that clearing has a strange effect on us. Once we're able to let go of our attachments to things and outcomes, and our buttons don't get pushed as much, we forget that we even had them!

You are not the same person you were when you started this book. In what ways do you feel that you have changed? Use the following questions to help you jiggle loose some awareness.

Have you noticed if . . .

- You're clearing, or have the urge to clear, more often?
- Your home or apartment feels different? Bigger? Lighter?
- You have attracted an opportunity, a new relationship, or greater financial ease?
- Your health, sleep patterns, eating patterns, or stress patterns have changed?
- Your relationship with a family member has changed?
- You have set and maintained clearer boundaries with others?
- Your sense of smell, taste, touch, sight, hearing, and/or inner knowing is heightened?
- You're more joyful—you're laughing more, having fun, and feeling in the flow?

- You've experienced some interesting synchronicities, pleasant surprises, dreams, shifts in perception, or aha moments?

Without judging any shifts as "good" or "bad," remember that in the greater scheme of things clearing anything, big or small, is about opening the channels to that place within that is uncomplicated and unplugged, sparkly and clear.

From the soul's point of view, our job is to evolve. The soul doesn't care if we're comfortable or not.

Explore
- Some of the ways I've changed . . .
- One significant change I've noticed since I began almost a year ago . . .

DAY 360
JUST BELOW THE SURFACE

The potential to achieve great things is just below the surface of our resistance to it.

What are you still resisting?

Can you say yes to your deep knowing? Even if it scares you?

Explore
- What I am still resisting . . .
- What I can say yes to (even if it scares me) . . .

DAY 361
YOUR TEACHERS

Use today to reflect on the lessons and clearing practices from this book that you found most challenging. Perhaps you wrote in your journal about the tasks that rattled your cage. That would be the place to start. These are your teachers.

Explore
- Some of the lessons and clearing practices I found most challenging this year are . . .
- I would like to (re-)declare my resolve to . . .

DAY 362
SHAKE IT UP

Think of your life as a sudsy bottle: The more you shake it up, the more suds come to the surface to be loved up and healed.

Sometimes you have to shake things up to uncover the shimmering essence of your true self.

What needs shaking up for next year? Today? Right now?

Explore
- What is shaking up for next year . . .
- What needs shaking up right now . . .

DAY 363
THIS IS IT

If there is one piece that summarizes the work of becoming our spacious selves, it would be this beauty by Lao Tzu:

Always we hope
Someone else has the answer.
Some other place will be better,
some other time
it will turn out.

This is it.
No one else has the answer.
No other place will be better,
and it has already turned out.

At the center of your being
you have the answer;
you know who you are
and you know what you want.

There is no need
to run outside
for better seeing.

Nor to peer from a window.

Rather abide at the center of your being;
for the more you leave it, the less you learn.

Search your heart
and see
the way to do
is to be.

Explore
- What I get from Lao Tzu's message . . . (and how it applies to me . . .)
- How I know that all the answers are within me . . . (Name and feel the part that still isn't so sure.)
- After nearly a year, these are some of the ways I have learned to *be* more and *do* less . . .

DAY 364
WISDOM FOR THE ROAD

As you journey forward into the heart of your own being, I offer you these parting reminders:

- Clutter is not the problem. It's how you relate to it that needs your love and attention.
- The only thing that is real—and really juicy—is happening right this second.
- Every moment is an opportunity to let go.
- You do not need fixing; the essence of who you are is not broken.
- Simplicity is the pathway to lasting change.
- Awareness changes everything.

Which of these truths speaks to you most right now? What can you do today to "bring it home"?

Explore
- The wisdom that most speaks to me right now . . .
- One thing I can do today to anchor it even more . . .

DAY 365
HAPPY NEW YOU!

Exactly a year ago, as I was finishing the online course on which this book is based, my husband came into my office and said, "Wow, Stephanie. Your eyes are really sparkly and clear!"

Guess what? This material has been working its magic on me too!

Whether it is through writing down words and/or acting on them, clearing has a way of doing that. When we slowly *drip, drip, drip* compassionate awareness into the places in our homes and lives that are stuck and out of balance, we change. For good.

I hope that you feel inspired to keep clearing every day in whatever small ways you can. Remember that consistency, not quantity, is the key to freedom and lasting change.

Consider these simple ways to continue the journey of cultivating a clear home and a spacious life:

1. **Go back to Day 1**. The more clearing you do, the more layers you'll peel away, and the more insights you'll gain. Though the messages will be the same, you won't be. Some of the messages may even feel completely new. That's because your internal lenses and filters are clearer!

2. **Connect with others.** Gather one or more friends, or invite your book group to join you in a six-week "clearing circle." Use this book as your guide and the interactive companion website, AYearToClear.com. If you need help starting a group, follow the steps in the appendix of *Your Spacious Self*, which offers simple guidelines and sample meeting agendas.

3. **Take an online course.** I have two courses on *DailyOM* that will guide you day to day. What you get there that you don't get in my books is a daily nudge in your email inbox,

audio meditations, and an opportunity to connect with others in the comment thread.

It has been an honor and a pleasure to join you on this pilgrimage. As we close this chapter for now, I leave you with a short contemplation:

When we tend our homes and lives in small ways, we take care of ourselves.

When we nourish ourselves, we bring ourselves back into balance.

When we restore balance, we bring peace to the world.

Happy trails, everyone! I'll see you on the path.

Acknowledgments

There are no words that adequately express how grateful I am. This book would simply not exist without the amazing beings who have inspired, supported, and walked with me on this journey.

To my Hierophant family: I could not have asked for a better publishing team to bring my 365-day "slow drip" vision into reality. Thank you, Randy Davila, for your generous spirit and willingness to take the long view with a book like this that can change the way people relate to clutter and clearing in their homes and hearts.

To my editor, Susie Pitzen: I am in awe of your ability to see and "clear" with eagle eyes. With a few strokes of your magic wand (I mean pen), you have smoothed out many rough edges, and brought out the spacious best of each lesson. To Allison Jacob: thank you for reading my manuscript in its infancy and sharing your valuable insights. To Emma Smith, what can I say? The cover is gorgeous.

To my friends and colleagues who have supported me in my quest to change the world one drawer at a time, thank you for your love and belief in me. A special thank you to Meg Hirshberg for your willingness to dig deeper into that thing you call a purse, and for suggesting that I devote a whole week on the subject. It was really fun deconstructing it! To April Eberhardt, my literary angel, thank you for your giddy enthusiasm and generous offerings of advice and inspiration. If every book had a favorite auntie, for this "baby," it would be you! To my San Miguel spirit sister, Nancy G. Shapiro, I am grateful for the girlfriend support, photos, e-cards, and beautiful reminders "to breathe, stretch, look out at the garden now and then, feed and hydrate [my] body so that I can feed and hydrate the world."

To all my readers and students: Thank you for trusting in a process that doesn't always add up, make sense, or go in a straight line. Your stories and testimonials are living proof that "going slow to let go" is infinitely more effective and satisfying (if not more fun) than going for the quick (fix).

To the students of my *DailyOM* **online courses**, "Clear Your Home, Clear Your Life" and "A Year to Clear What's Holding You Back!": You have moved me (often to tears) with your courage to clear what's holding you back and cultivate what is calling you forward. I am expanded and enriched every time I scroll down the comment thread to read your posts. Your stories, questions, fresh perspectives, and support of each other are a treasure: They inspire hope, lighten our load, and remind us that we are not alone in this journey. Thank you for being my teachers.

A special appreciation goes **to these writers and teachers, artists and poets, thought leaders and messengers**, who have inspired me, and whose wisdom graces the pages of this book: Abraham-Hicks, Brené Brown, Sophie Chiche, Pema Chödrön, Wayne Dyer, Elizabeth Gilbert, Seth Godin, Thich Nhat Hanh, Maira Kalman, Anne Lamott, Geri Larkin, Dr. Robert Maurer, Lynne McTaggart, Gunilla Norris, Madisyn Taylor, Iyanla Vanzant, Oprah Winfrey, and Desda Zuckerman. Thank you for helping us to slow down, think outside the box, see the beauty in all things, open up to creativity, embrace courage and imperfection, cultivate self-care, and become our best selves.

The stories I share in this book from my own life experience would be flat and colorless without the presence (presents) and participation of **the two big loves in my life**. To my beautiful redhead, **Camilla**: Your creativity, curiosity, and enthusiasm for life (and great food) inspires and lifts me every day. The world is a brighter place since you came into it twenty-four years ago. Thank you for reminding me how to play. To my beloved hubby, honey, and best friend of thirty years, **JV**: I am grateful every day for the opportunity to share this life with you. Thank you for making me laugh, being there when I cry, talking things through when I'm stuck, cheering me on when I'm strong. I could not have asked for a better partner to grow with and join me on this ride of a lifetime!

In the end, it is the personal stories woven into these pages, I believe, that give clearing its heart. It is our stories that connect and humanize us, that help us laugh and heal. **Thank you everyone** for shining your light and being a part of this great human adventure!

Books

Brown, Brené. *Daring Greatly: How the Courage to Be Vulnerable Transforms the Way We Live, Love, Parent, and Lead.* New York: Gotham, 2012.

———. *The Gifts of Imperfection: Let Go of Who You're Supposed to Be and Embrace Who You Are.* Center City, MN: Hazelden, 2010.

Chödrön, Pema. *When Things Fall Apart: Heart Advice for Difficult Times.* Boston, MA: Shambhala, 2002.

———. *Taking the Leap: Freeing Ourselves from Old Habits and Fears.* Boston, MA: Shambhala, 2010.

Kalman, Maira. *My Favorite Things.* New York: Harper Design, 2014.

Kondo, Marie. *The Life-Changing Magic of Tidying Up: The Japanese Art of Decluttering and Organizing.* Berkeley, CA: Ten Speed Press, 2014.

Lamott, Anne. *Small Victories: Spotting Improbable Moments of Grace.* New York: Riverhead, 2014.

Maurer, Robert. *One Small Step Can Change Your Life: The Kaizen Way.* New York: Workman, 2004.

Norris, Gunilla. *Being Home: A Book of Meditations.* Photographs by Greta D. Sibley. New York: Bell Tower, 1991.

Rumi, Jalal al-Din, *The Essential Rumi, New Expanded Edition.* Translations by Coleman Barks and John Moyne. New York: HarperOne, Reprint edition, 2004.

Tzu, Lao. *Tao Te Ching.* New York: Penguin, 1963.

Vogt, Stephanie Bennett. *Your Spacious Self: Clear the Clutter and Discover Who You Are.* San Antonio, TX: Hierophant Publishing, 2012.

Web Essays and Blog Posts

Seth Godin (editor), *What Matters Now*: http://sethgodin.typepad.com/seths_blog/2009/12/what-matters-now-get-the-free-ebook.html/.

Geri Larkin, "Close to the Ground: Just Stuff." *Spirituality & Health*, http://spiritualityhealth.com/articles/close-ground-just-stuff#main-content-top, July-August, 2014.

Anne Lamott, "Becoming the Person You Were Meant To Be: Where to Start." *O, The Oprah Magazine*, http://www.oprah.com/spirit/How-To-Find-Out-Who-You-Really-Are-by-Anne-Lamott.

Madisyn Taylor, "Your Comfort Zone: Create a Soft Place to Land" *DailyOM*, http://www.dailyom.com/articles/2007/6733.html.

Arianna Huffington, "Sleep Your Way to the Top." *Inc.*, http://www.inc.com/arianna-huffington/sleep-your-way-to-the-top.html.

Alice Park, "The Power of Sleep." *Time,* http://time.com/3326565/the-power-of-sleep.

Stephanie Bennett Vogt, "Lost and Found in Letting Go," *SpaceClear*, http://www.spaceclear.com/2010/04/lost-and-found-in-letting-go/.

Elizabeth Gilbert, "Ego vs. Soul." Facebook, https://www.facebook.com/GilbertLiz.

Online

A Year to Clear What's Holding You Back!; 365-Day Online Course by Stephanie Bennett Vogt; www.dailyom.com

Clear Your Home, Clear Your Life; 28-Day Online Course by Stephanie Bennett Vogt; www.dailyom.com

Svaroopa® yoga: Programs that develop a whole new capacity for movement, breath, and aliveness; http://svaroopa.org/yoga

Spacious images: www.pinterest.com/SpaceClear/

Stephanie Bennett Vogt; www.spaceclear.com

Videos

Kuenne, Kurt (writer, director, composer). "Validation." http://youtu.be/Cbk980jV7Ao?list=PLifyoA8MG3-6YPZKmagYHO_rDY8dKWe7V.

Stelar, Parov, "All Night." http://youtu.be/5ueJ4-lTa1s

Higa, Ryan. "First World Problems." http://youtu.be/vN2WzQzxuoA

"Do Nothing for 2 Minutes." http://www.donothingfor2minutes.com/

Resources

Visit the *A Year to Clear* website for updates and to connect with others on this journey:

www.AYearToClear.com

Follow us on Facebook and Twitter and receive daily inspirational messages:

www.facebook.com/SpaceClear
www.facebook.com/StephanieBennettVogt
www.twitter.com/SpaciousSelf

Learn more about Stephanie, her books, and inspirational programs designed to cultivate a clear home and a spacious life:

www.SpaceClear.com

About the Author

Stephanie Bennett Vogt is a leading space-clearing expert, international speaker, and the author of *Your Spacious Self: Clear the Clutter and Discover Who You Are.* She has taught her inspirational clearing programs at centers including Kripalu and the New England School of Feng Shui, and her work on simplifying, self-discovery, and letting go has appeared on the *Huffington Post* and *DailyOM* and in two anthologies: *Pearls of Wisdom* and *The Thought That Changed My Life Forever.* Stephanie and her husband divide their time between Concord, Massachusetts, and San Miguel de Allende, Mexico.

Hierophant Publishing
8301 Broadway, Suite 219
San Antonio, TX 78209
888-800-4240

www.hierophantpublishing.com